More Praise for *The Introverted Leader*

"Many of the most effective leaders are self-contained 'inner processors' who are nonetheless extremely capable of getting results. This book shows you how to get the most out of yourself and others whose management style is different."

—Brian Tracy, author of *The 100 Absolutely Unbreakable Laws of Business Success* and *Eat That Frog!*

"Kahnweiler believes that we must recognize the many thoughtful, inwardly focused, quiet 'gems' within our midst. If you count yourself as introverted some or all of the time, this book is a must-read."

—Liliana de Kerorguen, Vice President, Strategy and Business Development, Adams and Royer, Paris, France

"Introverts are often understated overachievers. Their quality and contributions may not be discovered and rewarded. If you are an introverted manager who finds public speaking intimidating and being around people draining, this book provides practical guidance that will help you embrace and control uncomfortable situations. It will enable you to be more effective."

—Ping Fu, President and CEO, Geomagic, and author of *Bend, Not Break*

"Jennifer B. Kahnweiler shows that she understands the challenges and opportunities introverted leaders face daily in a global marketplace. If you are an introverted leader or a manager of introverts — or both! — read this book. Kahnweiler delivers a proven four-part process drawn from her work in the trenches. Yes, introverted leaders can win!

—Fabrice Egros, President, UCB Pharma Inc.

"Does the thought of working a room make you want to run from the room? The good news is, you don't have to be the life of the party to be a successful leader. This book teaches people skills you can use to lead with confident, compassionate authority so you command the respect, loyalty, and results you want, need, and deserve. Read it and reap."

—Sam Horn, author of POP! and Tongue Fu!

"The Introverted Leader shows how to enhance your natural temperament and claim your place as an extraordinarily confident introverted leader in today's demanding workplace. Jennifer's strong track record of coaching the more reticent types among us shines through in this highly engaging and practical book."

—Dr. Tony Alessandra, coauthor of The New Art of Managing People and The Platinum Rule

"I've been an executive coach for more than fifteen years and only wish I'd had this book sooner for my many introverted clients. Jennifer's four-step process—clear, concrete, and centered on results—helps 'not-so-noisy' leaders avoid career derailment and achieve success. If you're an introvert—or you coach, mentor, or manage one—this is the book you've been waiting for. Buy it, read it, and put it to work!"

—Sharon Jordan-Evans, executive coach and coauthor of *Love 'Em or Lose 'Em*

"This is an important book for introverts and extroverts alike. Extroverts will benefit by gaining deeper insight into the mind of the introvert. Introverts will learn to embrace their introversion and the true value that they bring to the organizations they serve. The tips and tools that Kahnweiler introduces will help introverts navigate an extroverted corporate world. Shhh. Hear that? It's the sound of your confidence growing!"

—Bill Treasurer, founder of Giant Leap Consulting and author of *Courage Goes to Work*

"Jennifer B. Kahnweiler's experience with numerous high-level organizations speaks loud and clear in this first-of-its-kind book for introverted leaders. Those who are reluctant to step out of the shadows will learn to do so while keeping their personality intact."

—Tom Darrow, founder and Principal, Talent Connections, LLC

The
Introverted
Leader

The
Introverted
Leader

Building on Your
Quiet Strength

Jennifer B. Kahnweiler, Ph.D.

BK

Berrett–Koehler Publishers, Inc.
San Francisco
a BK Business book

Berrett-Koehler Publishers, Inc.
235 Montgomery Street, Suite 650
San Francisco, CA 94104-2916
Tel: (415) 288-0260 Fax: (415) 362-2512 www.bkconnection.com

Ordering Information

Quantity sales. Special discounts are available on quantity purchases by corporations, associations, and others. For details, contact the "Special Sales Department" at the Berrett-Koehler address above.

Individual sales. Berrett-Koehler publications are available through most bookstores. They can also be ordered directly from Berrett-Koehler: Tel: (800) 929-2929; Fax: (802) 864-7626; www.bkconnection.com

Orders for college textbook/course adoption use. Please contact Berrett-Koehler: Tel: (800) 929-2929; Fax: (802) 864-7626.

Orders by U.S. trade bookstores and wholesalers. Please contact Ingram Publisher Services, Tel: (800) 509-4887; Fax: (800) 838-1149; E-mail: customer.service@ ingrampublisherservices.com; or visit www.ingrampublisherservices.com/Ordering for details about electronic ordering.

Berrett-Koehler and the BK logo are registered trademarks of Berrett-Koehler Publishers, Inc.

Printed in the United States of America

Berrett-Koehler books are printed on long-lasting acid-free paper. When it is available, we choose paper that has been manufactured by environmentally responsible processes. These may include using trees grown in sustainable forests, incorporating recycled paper, minimizing chlorine in bleaching, or recycling the energy produced at the paper mill.

Library of Congress Cataloging-in-Publication Data

Kahnweiler, Jennifer B.
    The introverted leader : building on your quiet strength / Jennifer B. Kahnweiler.
        p. m
    Includes bibliographical references and index.
    ISBN 978-1-57675-577-8 (pbk. : alk. paper)
    ISBN 978-1-60994-200-7 (pbk. : alk. paper)
    1. Leadership. 2. Introverts. 3. Interpersonal communication. I. Title.
    BF637.L4.K27 2009
    155.2'32—dc22
                                        2009009339

First Edition

18   17   16   15   14   13   10   9   8   7   6   5   4   3   2   1

Production management: Publication Services. Cover design: Richard Adelson. Author photo: Josh Hobgood.

*To Lucille and Alvin Boretz,
parents extraordinaire,
who taught me the meaning
of love and laughter*

Contents

Foreword

by Douglas R. Conant

Every time I've taken a Myers-Briggs test, I've scored high on the introversion scale. As an introvert, I get energy from being by myself. I sometimes feel drained if I have to be in front of large groups of people I don't know for an extended period of time. And, as addressed in this book, people exhaustion takes its toll. After I've been in a social situation—including a long day at work—I need quiet time to be alone with my thoughts, reflect on the day, and recharge.

But as CEO of Campbell Soup Company, a company with nearly twenty thousand employees, I found myself particularly challenged because so much of my work required me to be "out there" in front of others. Not only that, I was also challenged to reverse a precipitous decline in market value—in a hurry. Over the course of my tenure, we succeeded in dramatically transforming the global leadership team, reconfiguring the portfolio, cutting costs, and making strategic investments in Campbell's products, marketing programs, innovation pipeline, and infrastructure. As a result, the company was able to deliver cumulative shareholder returns in the top tier of the global food industry.

Now, as founder and CEO of ConantLeadership, I have perhaps an even less introverted job. To help improve the quality of leadership in the twenty-first century, I often stand in front of a roomful of people and talk about how they, too, can be effective leaders in their organizations. One might ask how an introvert, like myself, makes this happen. Good question.

I'd be lying if I said that there wasn't a point in my life when I didn't aspire to be more outgoing, but it's just not in my nature. When I was nearly fifty, I began to realize that the best thing for me to do was to tell everyone with whom I worked the simple truth—I'm just shy. I realized that people are not mind readers—I needed to let them know what I was thinking and how I was feeling. Eventually, I developed this little talk, affectionately known as the "DRC Orientation," in which I shared with people the essence of who I was and what I was trying to do. I would tell it to new employees right off the bat. I did this so all the people with whom I worked would have a clear idea of who I am, where I come from, and what I expect everyone to do in order to succeed. I found that "declaring" my introversion was a very freeing exercise—more preferred than going through painful contortions in attempting to adapt to other people's styles. I have pursued this practice for well over ten years, and it really has helped me build strong relationships and quickly get beyond all the little superficial dances people do when they first start working with each other.

I have found that you need to make a conscious effort to develop your skill set. At one point in my career, the CEO of Nabisco wanted me to be president of the sales organization. I said, "You have got to be kidding me: (a) I'm an introvert, and (b) I can't play golf." Still, I ultimately accepted that position. I had to step even further out of my comfort zone, what Jennifer describes as the "push" component of her 4 P's Process. Emotionally, it was by far the most challenging job I've ever had, but I had to step up to the challenge. Making this stretch was necessary for me to grow as an effective leader and was very helpful in preparing me to become a CEO.

The Introverted Leader respects and honors the strengths introverts bring to the table and also offers a process whereby introverts gets results. Jennifer's 4 P's Process (preparation, presence, push, and practice) has been proven based on the tangible lessons she has gleaned from working with thousands of successful introverted leaders. This process provides introverts with a practical application for many challenging scenarios, from public speaking and networking to running a Fortune 500 company.

Both introverts and extroverts can learn from reading this book. Undoubtedly, introverts exist in all types of organizations. You simply can't overlook this entire group of contributors. Most people think of leaders as being outgoing, very visible, and charismatic people. I find that perspective to be overly narrow. You might just find that you have introverts embedded in your organization and, undoubtedly, some of them are natural-born leaders. The key challenge for leaders today is to get beyond the surface and unlock the full potential of all their colleagues. At times, extroverts may get to leadership positions faster, but for us introverts, it's all about working at our own pace and, at the end of the day, performing in a full way. Introverts can absolutely be extremely effective leaders; the landscape is full of excellent examples.

This book shows you how to increase your awareness and effectiveness in the workplace. If you are an extrovert, you will better understand and appreciate what your introverted teammates have to offer. If you are an introvert, you will gain insights and practical steps to build on your quiet strength. Ultimately, what helps all of us most is to embrace and fully leverage who we are in order to make the most substantial contributions possible. This book shows you how to do just that.

Douglas R. Conant
Former President and CEO of Campbell Soup Company
CEO, Conant Leadership

Preface

You talk when you cease to be at peace with your thoughts; And when you can no longer dwell in the solitude of your heart you live in your lips, and sound is a diversion and a past time.[1]

Kahlil Gibran

Someone said that work would be great, if it weren't for the people. Who hasn't felt that way at one time or another? Yet, workplace success is based on more than how much you know. It is equally about relationships with people. If you are an extrovert you are probably stimulated by the interpersonal interactions that build these relationships. However, in our outgoing, Type-A business culture, if you are an introvert who is more quiet in temperament, you may feel excluded, overlooked, or misunderstood. Your reticence might be mistaken for reluctance, arrogance, or even lack of intelligence. And perhaps you have found that your inconsistent people skills have caused your career to plateau. You're losing out on the career benefits that workplace relationships can provide. Your organization is also losing out on tremendous talent and expertise.

Yet, there is good news. Introversion can be managed. You can capitalize on a quieter, reflective demeanor and still adapt to a culture that rewards being "out there" and on stage. This book will show you how millions of people have succeeded in doing just that.

Who This Book Is For

Are you a mid-level or aspiring manager who has to influence others to get results? Perhaps you lead projects. Maybe you desire more responsibility and challenge in your role as an individual contributor. If you are a professional in a technical, scientific, or financial field, there is a strong likelihood that you have a quieter temperament. It is also probable that you have not been exposed to focused training in people skills like your counterparts in sales or management. You may be a woman in a male-dominated field or someone in a company who faces particular challenges in being heard.

You may view yourself as occasionally introverted. There are degrees of introversion, and occasions when even the "talkers" among us may be at a loss as to how to handle uncomfortable people situations. As a manager, of people or projects, it is likely you have introverts on your team. This book will help you learn to understand them, coach them, and maximize their contributions.

My Background

I confess. I am a strong extrovert. I talk out my thoughts, and I am the person many of you reading this may find "crazy making" at times. So, you ask, what would this "babbling brook" know about the world of introverts? Let me share a little background.

I have been a corporate consultant, speaker, and coach for more than 25 years. I have trained and counseled thousands of leaders across many organizations, and I have found introverted clients particularly receptive to the tools I share in this book. Many have followed up with specific examples of how they used techniques to get tangible results for themselves and their organizations. I am all for results.

As workplace columnist for *AARP The Magazine, The Society of Human Resources,* and the *Atlanta Journal Constitution* blog I have done extensive research on leadership success, including introverted leaders. In addition, the comments and questions I have received from readers deepened my understanding of the challenges and successes of quieter leaders.

And, finally, through my 35-year marriage to an introverted leader, I have developed empathy and admiration. I have learned to gain an appreciation for my husband Bill's quiet demeanor and his view of life. Looking through that lens has taught me so much about the value of quiet reflection.

The Approach

Tom was referred to me by a colleague. He was a twenty-something marketing manager who was interested in my research. He made a suggestion that I took to heart: "Don't listen to some loud mouth who is going to tell you to be like him because they don't know what it is like to be like me, do they? Motivational speaking is a billion dollar industry built on confident and extroverted people molding people into thinking they are wrong for being the way they are. Get advice from people who have dealt with the same problem." I decided to take his advice, so I personally interviewed and collected data from more than 100 introverted professionals across a wide range of industries. Some of these interviews were structured with set questions. Others were hallway conversations in client companies or conversations with interested airplane seatmates.

Wearing my journalist's hat, I observed team meetings, seminar discussions, and coaching sessions, looking for specific examples of how quieter leaders took charge. I filled notebooks with observations that were then incorporated into this book.

I found that posing specific questions on social networking sites also yielded rich responses. Many people preferred to communicate with me in writing. Their advice was rich and varied. *The Introverted Leader* also draws upon the unique perspectives of leading academics and business thinkers.

Book Overview

This book organizes information from all of these sources into a practical structure. Chapter 1, Four Key Challenges, lays out the challenges you face when you let yourself be ruled by ineffective introvert behaviors. You will learn how (1) stress, (2) perception gaps, (3) derailed careers, and (4) invisibility are significant hazards along the path to leadership.

Chapter 2, Unlocking Success: The 4 P's Process, describes a focused and practical method for breaking out of the status quo and effectively managing your introversion. The 4 P's Process (preparation, presence, push, and practice) serves as a road map to help you plan your strategy in a wide variety of leadership scenarios. You will also be able to use the 4 P's as a tool to continuously improve by analyzing what has been effective and not effective in your actions.

You will learn how (1) preparation means that you have a game plan and take the steps you need to prepare for people interactions; (2) presence means that you are able to fully be in the moment and "where your feet are"; (3) push means that you take deliberate risks and stretch yourself out of your comfort zone; and (4) practice means you continue to make these impact behaviors a part of your standing repertoire.

Chapter 3, Strengths and Soft Spots, includes a revealing quiz called *The Introverted Leadership Skills Quiz* that will help you recognize the behaviors you have already mastered in becoming an introverted leader. It will also assist you in zeroing in on the areas you may need to strengthen in order to fire on all cylinders. In addition, the quiz can serve as a baseline to assess your progress and a possible springboard for coaching discussions with your manager.

In chapters 4 through 9 you will learn how to apply the steps of the 4 P's Process to handle many typical work scenarios. A multitude of tools, specific examples, and practical tips will show you how to do this. Chapter 4, Public Speaking, will teach you how to gain mastery over presenting to groups and individuals. Chapter 5, Managing and Leading, shares many secrets from successful introverted leaders who have learned how to gain respect as leaders. Chapter 6, Heading Up Projects, focuses on the people side of project management. You will learn how introverted leaders can motivate the team to achieve strong results. Chapter 7, Managing Up, will prepare you with templates and tools to strengthen your partnership with your boss. Chapter 8, The Meeting Game, will take your involvement in meetings to a whole new level as you learn a multitude of ways to get your voice heard in the room.

Chapter 9, Building Relationships, addresses networking both in and outside the organization. As in the previous chapters, you will learn to capitalize on your introverted temperament to be both highly focused and creative in this essential leadership endeavor.

Chapter 10, Wins for You and Your Organization, addresses the many benefits both you and your organization will achieve when you build on your strengths and step out from behind the shadows.

Chapter 11, Going Forward, focuses on your next steps. Learning to moderate behaviors is certainly not a one-time event but a process that, like a fine wine, mellows and ages over time. You will find a development plan to help you zero in on achievable actions for now and the future as you adopt expanding leadership roles.

In addition to using the book, I encourage you to visit the Web site www.theintrovertedleaderblog.com. There you can download resources and connect with members of the introverted leader community in a fruitful, ongoing dialogue.

What Is an Introverted Leader?

Do you ever feel like extroverts get everything they ask for while your needs are passed over . . . or ignored?

Are you drained by business socializing?

Do you feel like you are not heard at meetings?

Have you ever turned down a speech or interview request?

If so, you may be introverted, and you are not alone. Many respected executives, such as Bill Gates, Warren Buffet, and Andrea Jung, are naturally introverted.[1] Other famous leaders, such as Mother Theresa, Abraham Lincoln, and Martin Luther King Jr., were thought to be introverted. The late Katharine Graham was introverted, and it is likely that President Barack Obama is an introvert. The list goes on.

A well-kept secret is that, like these well-known and successful introverts, there are millions of people who can experience deep discomfort and inhibition in interpersonal situations. This is not because there is something wrong with them. Introverts have a temperament that is more inner-focused, and they must adapt to an extroverted world, one that is primarily driven by interpersonal interactions. With estimates that almost 50 percent of the population[2] and 40 percent of executives are introverted, you are certainly not alone. Yet, to be an effective leader, you have a responsibility to connect with employees, customers, and colleagues and, like other successful introverted leaders, you need to find ways to succeed.

An Overview of Introversion and Extroversion

There is no one definition of introversion or extroversion that can be tied up neatly. However, it is an area of personality that can be

Figure 1. Typical Characteristics

Extroverts	Introverts
Energized by and seek out people; batteries "charged up" by other people	Energized by time alone; need time to "recharge" their batteries after interactions with other people
Talk first, think later	Think first, talk later
Talk out their thoughts	Process their thoughts in their head
Enthusiastic	Reserved
Are transparent, easy to read—like a fur coat with the fur on the outside	Less demonstrative emotion in facial expressions—like a fur coat with the fur on the inside
Freely share personal data with friends and strangers	Share personal data with a select few
Prefer talking to writing	Prefer writing to talking
Focus on breadth	Focus on depth

best explained by a description of general tendencies. If you haven't taken the Myers-Briggs Type Indicator (the MBTI) to determine your preference, doing a search online will reveal many resources to help you with this.

However, I find that most people seem to recognize their introversion when presented with some typical characteristics. Let's review the list above in Figure 1 and see which side resonates with you more.

If you are torn between both sides of the chart, it is not a problem. You might ask yourself the question, "If I had to be one for the rest of my life, which one would I choose?" Some people have situational introversion. There are certain scenarios in which they reveal introverted tendencies. It is said that even Oprah Winfrey was tongue-tied when she met Nelson Mandela for the first time!

There is a difference between introversion and shyness. Shyness is driven by fear and social anxiety. Although the symptoms may overlap (e.g., avoidance of public speaking), introversion is a preference and should not be considered a problem.

Can Introverts Be Leaders?

Absolutely, introverts can be successful leaders. I define leaders very broadly. If you are someone who recognizes that you need to work through people to achieve results, then you are a leader. If you are not satisfied with the status quo and want to improve processes and make a difference, then you are a leader. If you want to help people, then you are a leader. I leave it up to you to define the term for yourself. Leaders have to make sure the job gets done, and they also need to plan for change, coach others, and work with other people to get results.

There is a strong case to be made for the success of introverted leaders. *Good to Great* by Jim Collins has become a classic business book. In studying the characteristics of successful companies, Jim Collins found that every successful company he studied had a leader who exhibited what he called "Level 5" characteristics during times of transition. They demonstrated a focus on results, but equally important, and perhaps paradoxically, they each possessed personal humility. They displayed "compelling modesty, were self-effacing and understated"[3]; these qualities and this emotional intelligence seem very aligned with the introverted leader.

In a study published in *CIO Magazine*,[4] senior executives said that a lack of empathy was a key cause of failure in leaders today. These results match research that was done by the guru of emotional intelligence, Daniel Goleman. He found that the best bosses have something called high social intelligence. This form of intelligence correlates more with attention and focus on relationships. Those with high social intelligence are able to connect with others and greatly influence the performance of their people.[5]

How Leaders Manage Their Introversion

Turn a Weakness into a Strength

In my consulting with successful business executives over the years, I have found many who have been candidly honest about being introverted. In fact, they tend to talk about the topic at length, as though they have never been asked about this "secret." They approach introversion as they would any other challenging business problem and seek to understand which behaviors are working and which aren't. Then they develop a strategy and execute a plan.

The successful introverted leader actually turns what might be considered a weakness into a strength. One well-respected manager was given feedback in his career that he was too "low key." In his future role as a senior leader he turned this laid-back persona into presence. He had a strong ability to project a calm confidence—a sense of ease, poise, and self-assurance that transferred to all the people around him.

Another leader turned her disdain for large-group socializing into a chance to get her vision across to her team in different ways. She made a point of building on her preference for one-on-one conversations. As a result, she got to know each of her people, and she built clear communication channels and trust.

These leaders have found creative ways to adapt. In and out of diverse workplaces, one-on-one and in groups, the ongoing give and take with customers and colleagues is what gets results and ultimately makes the difference in whether or not you are a credible and respected leader, colleague, and employee.

Though she is far from a role model, Miranda Priestly, the ghastly boss (and "closet introvert" perhaps?) in the film *The Devil Wears Prada* uses a technique that serves her well. Her two assistants memorize the names, photo headshots, and trivia about all of her party guests, which they then unobtrusively whisper in her ear before each encounter.

One CEO I interviewed said that he managed his anxiety in meetings with subordinates by taking careful notes, not realizing how incredibly helpful this would be when he needed this information months later.

The power of silence is another characteristic that can serve as a strength. Many people are not comfortable with silence and try to fill the gaps with comments that are off the cuff, whereas the comments made by the introvert can be more thoughtful. Sid Milstein,

VP Global BPO for EDS, an HP company, told me that you can convey a sense of reflective wisdom to your peers and your bosses because you "hopefully, are considering facts and issues before speaking."

Introverts can access greater wisdom from within when their mind is quiet. They can choose their words carefully and correctly. An executive coach I know who has worked with many senior executives said that when these reflective leaders speak, what shows up is very powerful. Judy Gray, president and CEO of the Florida Society of Association of Executives said, "The whole phenomenon of quiet yet effective leadership deserves to be recognized and appreciated. The passionately exuberant or charismatic leader initially has a leg up on capturing people's hearts and minds, but those characteristics alone are not what create sustainable progress or meaningful change." A really powerful, astute Ivy-League type years ago told her, "The person in the room with the most power is the quietest."

Pausing and reflecting also helps keep introverted leaders from putting their feet in their mouths. One person I spoke with who works in politics expressed gratitude at being able to hold his tongue. Where he worked, one wrong word could have cost him his job.

When you are introverted, you also have more time to observe and read people. Mary Toland, a senior project manager, has been able to groom talent on her project team by coaching those who have receded into the background. She has developed empathy for introverted, emerging leaders, and shares a realistic view of what it takes to rise in the ranks and succeed in her organization. Mary is now passing this knowledge on.

This book will show you the many ways you can adapt your leadership style now and in the future. Just as you may complete Sudoku puzzles or learn a new language to stretch your brain, you can gain practical and proven tools to build on your quiet strength. The next chapter will clarify the tangible challenges you will likely experience as you move down the road toward being a successful introverted leader.

Chapter 1

Four Key Challenges

"It's not easy being green," sang Kermit the Frog on *The Muppet Show*. Substitute "introverted" for "green." Although you may have buzzed along pretty smoothly in your role as individual contributor, once you decide to move your career forward, or after your organization taps you for more responsibility, life can become more complex if you are withdrawn.

Let's look at key challenges that can result from being an introverted professional.

The Challenges

Understanding what challenges can occur in your life as an introvert at work helps you realize what behaviors to change. We tend to make adjustments when the pain of doing things the same old way is great enough. When we encounter roadblocks while driving, we are forced to find alternative routes. Similarly, these workplace barriers can be enlightening. A number of my introverted coaching clients have had light bulbs go off when we have discussed the following four common challenges. Giving a name to what they've experienced often gives them an impetus to change. Let's look at the four major categories of challenges introverted leaders encounter at work. They are (1) stress, (2) perception gaps, (3) career derailers, and (4) invisibility.

1. Stress

Work overload, physical symptoms, and people exhaustion are all negative consequences that can hit introverts hard in the workplace. Here are some examples of each.

Work Overload

Recently out of school, a woman I know named Mady landed a plum job as a staff accountant at a large health care organization. She was looking forward to learning a lot and using her education. The honeymoon period of the first few weeks flew by, and her manager was pleased with her work. Unfortunately, a few weeks later, the picture had changed dramatically. Mady was getting into the office at 6:30 A.M. and leaving after 7:00 P.M. Her schedule was causing friction with her boyfriend and friends.

What happened in the interim? Mady had been pulled onto a few projects, and word got out that she was a sharp employee. When asked to join a project, she didn't say no. Afraid that people would think she was not capable or willing, Mady ended up drowning in a sea of projects and deadlines. In the end, she struggled to deliver on all her commitments. Her boss was not even aware of all her work, or he might have put the brakes on his overeager employee.

Have you ever found yourself unable to say no to a work request? For introverted people, lacking the self-assurance and confidence to assert themselves in social situations can affect not only their performance, but even more importantly, their health. It is not as much stress (which will always be there) but our reaction to it that causes problems. Mady's inability to set limits and ask for some direction from her boss created work/life balance issues that were destined to get worse.

Physical Symptoms

At a recent seminar, I was talking with two withdrawn men who both acknowledged that they stuttered at meetings when called on to speak. In more relaxed surroundings, like the class, they were fine, but in this work situation they froze up. These participants illustrated that there is most likely a mind-body connection to stress. Symptoms like headaches, stomachaches, and back problems can also be correlated with stress reactions. Even the awkwardness that introverted people sometimes feel with people can take its toll. Holding feelings inside when we are frustrated makes it highly likely that these types of physical symptoms will occur.

People Exhaustion

It is also common for introverted leaders to become very tired when they are forced to continually be with people. Fatigue and a sense of dread can set in before a social event, and these get-togethers are endured with clenched teeth. One of my introverted colleagues left a convention a day early because of her exhaustion from being around "so many happy, talkative people." Another asked me if I had heard the joke about the introverted manager who said he would rather stay home with a bad book that he had already read than face one of those awful cocktail receptions.

One of the ways you can tell if you are introverted is that you need time to recharge your batteries and decompress after you spend time with others. The author of *Mars and Venus in the Workplace*, John Gray, PhD, portrays a "cave" as a metaphor for a man's place of retreat, where he can take a needed break from the opposite sex.[1] Many introverts tell me that a similar type of escape is essential to recover from the utter exhaustion they feel from being surrounded by extroverts.

I have some empathy. I was on a relaxing beach vacation recently when one of the hotel guests caused me to experience a stress reaction. He seemed like a nice guy at the beginning of our conversation. After he did not shut up for the next 45 minutes, and after I tried several times to interject a comment or a question, I felt tired and not heard. This is what I believe introverts must feel daily.

Sometimes, being surprised can create stress. Paul Otte, an IT project manager at IBM with more than 15 years of experience, said that he experiences stress when he is called on to respond quickly and does not have an answer. He described it as feeling "naked." He worries most about the people he calls "snipers," the folks who use some esoteric piece of data to discredit his point.

Forcing yourself to play a visible management role can also take its toll. Being outgoing, conversational, and engaged is something that Sid Milstein does as a leader. He also finds that he can become mentally exhausted from the role playing, not the discussion. Sid told me, "It can take the form of a headache, the need to be alone to reflect upon 'what I've just done.' It's no different than what I might feel after a physical workout. . . . Of course in the continuing acting role, I have to disguise this from everyone else, which keeps my stress level up." Adapting their behavior can become easier over time, but it will never be their natural style. Introverted professionals have to be self-aware on a continual basis, and this takes a great deal of energy.

2. Perception Gaps

There are often key differences between how we think people see us and how they actually do. You have heard the phrase, "perception is reality." In his book *Cracking the Code*, Thom Hartman says, "The meaning of communication is the response you get."[2] It can be helpful for introverted professionals to understand the nature and results of this disconnect between their intended message and what comes across. Negative impressions, and possibly being labeled as slow thinkers or as having no backbone are some of the negative perceptions that introverted leaders may face. Let's take a closer look at each of these.

Negative Impressions

Introverted people do not intend to create a negative impression. Yet, they often do with others who are more outgoing. They want to be seen as competent and confident in their work environments, but along the way, this can get derailed. Their silence and sparse words can create the impression that they are withdrawn, gruff, insensitive, or even rude. This prompts others to ask, "What's wrong?" when introverts don't feel that anything is the matter. Jonathon Rauch wrote a terrific article for *The Atlantic Monthly* called "Caring for Your Introvert."[3] He said that introverts are often asked if they are okay, and also told they are too serious. He went on to discuss the disconnect between extroverts and introverts in this way: "Extroverts have little or no grasp of introversion. They assume that company, especially their own, is always welcome. They cannot imagine why someone would need to be alone; indeed they often take umbrage at the suggestion. As often as I have tried to explain the matter to extroverts, I have never sensed that any of them really understood. They listen for a moment and then go back to barking and yipping. Impressions are formed early on in a relationship and though they don't intend to be seen as angry or curmudgeons, introverted people are often perceived this way. Unfortunately, these impressions tend to stick."

Self-expression can also lead to misunderstandings in others. *The Infinite Mind,* a radio show on public radio, covered the topic of shyness in a recent episode. Though shyness is associated with a lack of confidence and anxiety, and is different from introversion, the following comment is still relevant. One of the subjects interviewed spoke of having a distinctive voice that people commented on: "All of a sudden I knew that they noticed something about me. And I guess it's that feeling of being noticed. It's like people getting the wrong impression. People don't really understand who you are because your outside presents something very different. But inside, you could be really strong, very aware, and very bright, and . . . because you are a little bit introverted or intimidated you come across as this fumbling, kind of high-voiced silly girl."[4]

In the absence of words, sinister assumptions can be formed by others and projected onto the quiet person. One introvert found that others on his IT work team thought that he was plotting some scheme and manipulating the boss. Why? It was simply because he was quiet at meetings. The office politics became pretty ugly, and misunderstandings accumulated from this wrong perception.

Slow Thinkers

Another misperception is that introverted people lack quick thinking. If they don't share their ideas *immediately* they are not seen as contributors. Martin Schmidler, vice president, information technology at a food service distribution company, shared comments representative of many introverts. "I like to listen, hear all the facts, all the different points of view and I like to process them." He went on to say that often, pausing to offer a carefully considered response can be perceived as either not being quick enough, being a procrastinator, or even being indecisive, a major faux pas for those on the leadership track. People who listen first are seen as not being able to think on their feet, another major liability in many organizational cultures. Martin, by the way, did learn to close this perception gap by taking deliberate steps addressed later in this chapter.

No Backbone

Quieter people can also be seen as weak, with no backbone, especially when many leaders around them adopt more aggressive stances. Others are jockeying for position, and when the introvert does not push back, the more reserved personality can easily be manipulated. As a result, you may get assigned roles you didn't choose and, like Mady, who was described earlier, an overloaded plate. Unless you develop more assertive behaviors, this pattern continues and can make it very difficult for you as a quieter individual to be seen as a strong leader.

3. Career Derailers

It requires more than technical or subject matter expertise to get people motivated and achieve results. Interpersonal skills are key as you take on leadership roles. When you are achieving results for your company *and* developing relationships, career possibilities open up both in your organization and in your field. Introverted people inevitably hit a wall in their careers when they don't attend to the relationships side of the equation. These "soft skills," as they used to be called, are now taking center stage as necessary competencies. Hence, there has been tremendous investment in training and coaching for professionals, and leadership development programs have mushroomed in recent years. Some career derailers are the undersell, missed connections, avoiding politics, and working harder not smarter.

The Undersell

Careers are made or broken by what people know about you and your accomplishments. Southerners in the United States have an expression, "Don't brag on yourself." In other words, be humble. Unfortunately, the world of work doesn't go by these rules. You can't expect people to be mind readers, so by not highlighting the results you have obtained, you can stay stagnant in your role. Other missed opportunities may include promotions, choice assignments, and opportunities to do something that is new and different. Sid Milstein said, "An extrovert might easily sell themselves in a favorable light, but I keep waiting for that phone call."

If you don't talk about what you do, people don't know about either your skills or your potential. So, if you don't "brag on yourself," you can miss out on the challenging job and project opportunities that occur in fluid organizational structures.

When project leaders are looking for the right person to take charge, you are not on their radar screen. It can also have serious consequences for your career progression. Not selling themselves was a an often-lamented regret of the people I interviewed for this book.

Missed Connections

"It is not what you know, but who you know," goes the old expression. This still rings true today. Mary Toland said a missed opportunity to build relationships earlier in her career greatly impacted her career progression. She didn't realize until later that it would make sense to stop in and chat with her bosses about their families, sports, etc. In her company's culture, it was important to forge relationships to further your career.

People hire people they know and trust. I joined one organization that discouraged the exchanging of business cards at events. Members got to know each other through working together on projects in the community. From that type of real experience of interacting with each other, you learned whether you wanted to engage in business together. Today, I consider some of these folks (a number of introverts among them) key members of my own personal advisory board.

If you are hesitant to branch out of your comfort zone, and fail to expand your network in and out of work, you will never forge the kind of relationships that make you a visible and valuable asset to your organization and profession.

Avoiding Politics

Most people think of office politics as a negative, nasty game. Gossip, rumors, innuendo, and backstabbing are certainly part of the mix. For quieter people, laying low can keep them focused and more productive, especially during times of crisis. However, much of the political game is natural and not necessarily negative.

Politics (the good kind) is also about putting political capital in the bank, where it builds with compound interest over time. This means connecting with the right people, who are not necessarily the most senior members of the organization, but are often the people others respect and who are well-networked themselves. Making deposits of this political capital involves spending time with these people, finding out their critical priorities and needs, and determining where the organization is headed. Learning more about the culture from your network helps you to craft your goals.

Working Harder Not Smarter

I teach management seminars for mid-level and aspiring leaders. The seminars, which cover communication and business skills, are typically filled with professionals who deal with data or information. People come from areas such as accounting, finance, engineering, and IT. They are researching pharmaceuticals that may save members of my family. They are planning bridges and helping their companies stay in compliance with complex regulations. Most are high performers, or their companies would not be investing thousands of dollars a year in their development. They are not slackers. However, many lack critical people skills.

Are you occasionally getting out of your cube like the extroverts do in order to have these critical conversations? Many introverts avoid these relationship-building discussions altogether. It is natural to retreat to your office, or if you are telecommuting, to rarely check in. Avoiding people and working hard at your job can be effective for a while. In many fast-paced organizations, where lots of interpersonal interaction is required, it can take so much energy that little is left to devote to the job. Being an "actor," as many introverts have expressed, takes everything you have. As one person told me, "It is painful sometimes to put on a happy face." We only have a certain amount of energy. If you don't learn effective ways of getting comfortable being with people, then you come to work geared up for battle, tensed up, and just trying to survive the day. With this approach, it is highly likely that your performance will be affected. When the next promotion, or new and exciting assignment, comes around, it very well may not be yours.

4. Invisibility

Not being front and center is another trait that can create problems for introverts in the workplace. The key impacts of being invisible are lost opportunities, ideas not heard, and lost personal power.

Lost Opportunities

The "shiny" extroverted person will often get the resources he needs to do his job while his more introverted co-worker sits back in frustration. This may happen even if the extroverted person is all show. Laurie Nichols, CEO of a successful nonprofit organization, said, "These people are all fluff and no stuff." Despite the fact that the introvert is plugging away, he may not be getting the credit for his work. When it comes time for budget allocations, pay raises, or plum assignments, guess who loses out? Management tends to overlook the strengths, capabilities, and accomplishments of the introverted person when these folks are not taking center stage.

One young introverted leader in public relations has noticed that meetings in his company are a place where perceptions are formed. He believes they make a huge difference in your future and thinks that the relationships that are cultivated in this group setting lead to impressions that are formed by higher management. Because he hasn't been one to "throw it around," he believes that he is not getting some choice assignments even though he is completing those types of tasks quickly and efficiently. "People know you are there but you are not holding the banner."

Remaining in the background in these situations is similar to looking for work in a city where you don't live. When you are out of sight it is much harder to be "top of mind" to employers. In organizations people forget that you are there. The result can be a demotivating cycle in which you become frustrated from not getting rewards. You are not sure what you need to do, aside from turn your temperament upside down.

Ideas Not Heard

Because introverts tend to be more laid back, their insights, ideas, and solutions can fly under the radar. Introverted clients have often told me that they are unable to find a slot in which to insert their ideas, particularly in group discussions. In one-on-one dialogue with extroverts, they also have a hard time interjecting their comments and being heard. Many scratch their heads and sense that their slower, more deliberate style may be the culprit. They complain that even when they do have a chance to speak up, their ideas are either passed over or co-opted by the more aggressive types on their team.

Laurie Nichols described a frustrating experience that created stress for her and the other quieter individuals in a high-profile leadership program. "The extroverts really dominated the air space every time we got together. . . . It was a dog and pony show for them. Every time I would try to insert myself into the group discussion, I would be interrupted by an extrovert who would then redirect the conversation. . . . I was suffering from introversion." Fading into the woodwork is an experience many other introverted leaders have highlighted.

Some also complain of their ideas not sticking. A seasoned IT leader at IBM told me that his natural style is to reflect on ideas quietly and then send out an e-mail with his carefully considered responses. He finds that he has not been particularly effective in getting his ideas heard. Even poorly designed proposals that get floated in a public forum seem to have more staying power than those sent out in e-mails later on. In his organization, you are judged more by your verbal than written input.

Lost Personal Power

In addition to reducing influence in corporate discussion and decision making, being invisible can cost personal power and influence.

I recently learned of a particularly frustrating situation that affected an introverted team leader. Apparently, he needed some reporting data from each person on the team by a certain date, and he let them know this via e-mail. When he didn't receive the information, he wrote a nasty e-mail to the team berating them for their lack of compliance, also telling them that they didn't care about the project. Had he checked with the group by phone or in person, he would have found that the system required to obtain the data had broken down and was causing the delay.

E-mail has been called a "multiplier of misunderstandings." Though e-mail has been a boon for introverts, it can also create numerous disconnects, and sour just the relationships you need to build to succeed as a leader.

For example, as a result of this manager's e-mail follow-up, his team is pretty soured on him, and I suspect he will continue to have a challenging time keeping them on board with the work ahead. By making faulty assumptions about their attitude and lack of compliance, he relinquished any personal power he might have had.

Awareness Helps

The challenges discussed in this chapter can feel daunting at times, but the good news is that you can and will deal with these detours. If you know they lie ahead you can prepare for them and turn potential obstacles into opportunities to change, and then you will become an even stronger leader than you already are.

The next step is taking action. Let's talk about how to turn these challenges into opportunities by using a practical process called the 4 P's.

Chapter 2

Unlocking Success: The 4 P's Process

The 4 P's Process

There is no magic to managing introversion, but there are tangible steps you can take to address challenges and turn them into opportunities. The 4 P's Process is an easy-to-remember road map to improve your performance. Preparation, presence, push, and practice address the four challenges of stress, perception gap, derailed careers, and invisibility. These steps include many tools to move you forward as an introverted leader. If you are a manager of introverts, you can use the 4 P's as a coaching tool. The 4 P's will also be useful if you are a team member who wants to better communicate with your introverted colleagues.

Use the 4 P's Process as a barometer to track your progress and to reflect on both successful and noneffective interactions. It can also help you to plan what you might do differently in the next upcoming scenario.

How It Works

The 4 P's Process includes four components: *preparation, presence, push, and practice* (see Figure 2). Preparation is the first step in the cycle. Even if you enter a leadership scenario as an introvert, preparation will give you the confidence to handle any spontaneous situation. Presence, the second step, is how you are positioned in the present. It is the step that shows people you are engaged. The third step in the process is push. This is the step in which you push yourself out of your comfort zone. Pushing through your fear, after you

Figure 2. The 4 P's Process

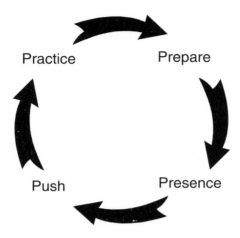

Practice   Prepare

Push   Presence

have prepared and learned ways of being present, is the way to develop and solidify your skills. The fourth step is practice. It is taking advantage of every opportunity to practice new behaviors. It is what great champions continue to do on a daily basis. After you have mastered a skill or a tool, the 4 P's process starts all over again. There is always a new scenario to be addressed. Let me give you some more examples of how my clients and interviewees have used these steps.

Preparation

Preparing for interpersonal interactions is the single best action step you can take. We often think we can "wing it" in conversations, in presentations, and with challenging people. The opposite is true. If you give the same attention and focus to strategizing for interpersonal interactions as you do to projects, then great things can happen. *Stress* is reduced, and the *perception gap* closes.

   Have you ever prepared for a tough meeting by anticipating questions and writing down your possible answers? How about role playing with a friend? You probably felt more on top of your game and confident when you entered that conference room. When you were thrown questions you hadn't prepared for, you could draw from your reservoir of recently reviewed knowledge to craft a strong answer. If so, then you know what a difference reviewing things beforehand can make. Numerous examples were given to me by successful introverted leaders I spoke with, and they all involved preparation. Many of those examples of conscious preparation are included throughout *The Introverted Leader.* Here are two quick examples now.

The young PR leader mentioned earlier finds that a good buffer for his anxiety before presentations is to prepare extensive notes, including specific phrases he will use. He finds that if he writes these down beforehand, he is able to mentally bring up the entire paragraph when he glances down, and he adds, "I can get through it without any introversion getting in the way." Martin Schmidler, IT leader, was recently at an important networking event. He was able to gain access to the seating chart and studied it seriously to identify key clients whom he could target at the large cocktail reception. Preparation was the key to reducing his anxiety, and it helped him secure a large account.

Preparation means you have a game plan, so take the necessary time to be alone and strategize for interpersonal interactions (e.g., clarify your purpose, think of specific questions and phrases to say, take notes, and rehearse with a trusted peer). Observe those who have great interpersonal skills and integrate their approaches into your style. It works.

Presence

The dictionary defines presence as "a person's bearing especially when it commands respectful attention." If you are prepared, you can relax and "be here now." Many introverted leaders overprepare, and then go with the flow. One of the best ways to demonstrate leadership is to show that you are present. A friend said of a person she admired, "When he was with you, he was *with* you." The *perception gap,* or the gap between your intended image and your perceived image, substantially closes if your listener believes that you are with them.

Instead of being perceived as an aloof or disconnected person, you are viewed as someone who has empathy and integrity.

By focusing on the current moment and the person you are with, you also build rapport and personal power. I remember meeting the COO of a company I had recently joined. I admittedly was intimidated, as she was a person of influence who was several reporting levels above me. I also had a number of complex job challenges facing me in the days ahead, and I wanted to make a positive impression. In chatting with her as we waited for a meeting to begin, I immediately relaxed. She looked straight at me and asked intelligent questions that showed *sincere* interest. Though there were many more senior people around, I felt as though I was the only one in the room. I had her complete attention. I never forgot that first conversation. In subsequent encounters, she demonstrated presence by seeking to understand my needs and offering reasoned guidance. Her behavior made all the difference in my motivation to do the best job possible.

When you show presence, you are also more authentic, which is another essential component of leadership. Consider this scene from *The Pursuit of Happyness*.[1] Chris Gardner, the homeless character played by Will Smith, came into his stockbroker intern interview wearing ragged clothes. He had been sleeping in jail all night because he hadn't paid traffic tickets. Instead of relying on his "prepared answers," he assessed his situation and decided to tell the truth. This was a risky move, but one that resulted in admiration and ultimately a job offer.

Introverted leaders who have developed presence also consciously *prepare* for unanticipated happenings. They have thought about backup topics when the conversation stalls. They have generic open-ended questions up their sleeve and call forth stress-reduction techniques such as remembering to breathe when faced with challenges. The late Dr. Fred Otte, a professor admired by many in his field, was a very introverted person. In discussing this book with his widow Jennifer Bush, I learned that one backup technique that Fred used in social settings was to tell stories he had ready to pull out at any time. She said that if someone was droning on, he would be sure to tell a story to get himself energized and in the moment. His boring colleague would be none the wiser, and Fred maintained his strong reputation as a genuinely nice guy.

Push

Emerson said, "Do that which you are most afraid to do." Much has been written about how we have to push past our fears to overcome them. This is easier said than done; yet many of the introverted leaders I spoke with did take deliberate steps to push themselves out of their comfort zones and into uncomfortable interpersonal interactions. When you push yourself to take risks, you allow others to see what your potential is. Careers can get back on track when you push yourself. Your *career will accelerate.* When Mary Toland forced herself to build a relationship with her boss, she saw her career move forward. You are no longer *invisible,* and you gain key opportunities when you push. When Martin Schmidler pushed himself to grab the seating chart and mingled with a purpose, he secured a key client account.

Another CIO I knew pushed himself by answering a challenge from his coach, who told him that he was to collect 20 business cards at an upcoming 30-minute cocktail reception they attended. He forced himself to do just that and eventually became known as an expert networker in his organization.

It is important to place yourself in situations where you are forced to stretch and get out of your comfort zone, whether it be public speaking or having a difficult conversation with a customer. One introverted leader made the best case for pushing past discomfort when he said, "You still want to know what you can do in this world."

Practice

Practice is the final step in the 4 P's Process. Practice will make you proficient and help you incorporate many tools into your standing repertoire—it is the difference in the golf swing of champions such as Tiger Woods, who practice continually despite their champion status. It is practice that keeps you fresh and experimenting with different ways to connect with people and deliver your message. Practice is also what gives you the ability to recalibrate your approach and demeanor depending on the situation.

Here is another way to look at this step. Let's say you are right-handed. If you break that hand, you will use your left hand to go about your daily tasks. It will most likely feel awkward at first, but after a while, you will be reasonably competent. Are you totally at ease and stress free? No, you are not using the hand you normally use. However, over time, your use of it will feel more fluid.

As in the hand scenario, when you practice *behaviors* at work that are unnatural, they will feel strange at first. However, with conscious repetition, you learn to close the perception gap by being viewed as who you want to be. Trust and credibility will increase with co-workers, direct reports, and your bosses. By taking down the cloak of invisibility, you will be moving your career forward.

In the chapters ahead, I will show you how to take low-risk opportunities to *practice* in a wide range of typical workplace scenarios. If you follow these suggestions, you will increase both your skill and your confidence.

Chapter 3

Strengths and Soft Spots

Sean was pleased with his promotion from team lead to manager, and the first few weeks went smoothly. There were lots of pats on the back and a nice raise, but nothing much else changed. He was still in there as a team member, pushing up against deadlines, scrambling to meet customer needs, etc. One day his boss came down to see him with concerns about deliverables that were missing. He then gave Sean a quick coaching lesson about the expectations of his new role. Sean, he said, needed to move from being a hands-on player to a leader—to get out there motivating his folks and inspiring high performance. His focus needed to shift from the task he was performing to the people he was leading.

Over several months, Sean learned to get "out of the sandbox" with his team, and he had more time to respond to his team's and management's needs. He maintained his quiet demeanor but adapted his style to meet the new challenge he faced. It was a learning process for Sean, and he ended up excelling as a leader, grateful to the boss who pushed him to take charge.

Have you ever, when stretched to perform, discovered capacities that you never knew existed? This often happens with leaders who are introverted. They don't seek promotions. Until pushed out of their comfort zone, they often see themselves as technically competent but not as people who can profoundly influence others. Yet when offered an opportunity to take charge, introverted individuals can lead with a presence more powerful than their more talkative counterparts. This feeling is "catching" to the people around them, and can set the stage for a department to exceed expectations, and ultimately for a company to achieve strong results.

Most experts on human behavior conclude that our temperaments are shaped by a combination of both genes and environmental influences. It is not a question of nature or nurture, but how these two elements interact with each other. Sean had a quiet, laid-back temperament. His previous experience contributed to his view of how a manager was supposed to manage. Adding new skills to his leadership palette through his boss's mentoring allowed him to move outside of some learned behaviors while still being true to his own style.

Leadership Skills—A Quiz for Introverts

So what about you? Are you firing on all cylinders? What skills do you need to learn to make you more powerful as an introverted leader? Take a few minutes to complete this brief quiz (see Figure 3). It will help you identify areas to focus on as you read the chapters ahead.

Figure 3. Introverted Leadership Skills Quiz

Circle your responses based on your own assessment of yourself at work. Try not to be too tough or too easy on yourself.

SA = Strongly Agree

A = Agree

D = Disagree

SD = Strongly Disagree

NA = Not Applicable

I. Public Speaking

1. I prepare stories and examples for my presentations.	SA	A	D	SD	NA
2. I rehearse presentations out loud.	SA	A	D	SD	NA
3. I use my voice for maximum impact.	SA	A	D	SD	NA
4. I take opportunities to speak publicly for practice.	SA	A	D	SD	NA

II. Managing and Leading

1. I maintain an appropriate balance
   of hands-on work and delegation.   SA   A   D   SD   NA

2. I consider personal and
   communication styles when
   managing.   SA   A   D   SD   NA

3. I am fully present and tuned in
   when listening.   SA   A   D   SD   NA

4. I let conflict surface on my teams
   when necessary.   SA   A   D   SD   NA

III. Heading Up Projects

1. I spend time building credibility with
   project members.   SA   A   D   SD   NA

2. I am clear in informing people about
   my expectations for a project.   SA   A   D   SD   NA

3. I share the limelight with others on
   projects.   SA   A   D   SD   NA

4. I use humor to stimulate creativity
   and teamwork on projects.   SA   A   D   SD   NA

IV. Managing Up

1. I meet with my boss on a regular
   basis.   SA   A   D   SD   NA

2. I prepare questions for him/her about
   roles and goals.   SA   A   D   SD   NA

3. I approach my boss with problems
   and potential solutions.   SA   A   D   SD   NA

4. I give and receive feedback from
   my boss.   SA   A   D   SD   NA

V. The Meeting Game

1. I prepare agendas for meetings and
   ask for an agenda when I am invited
   to a meeting.   SA   A   D   SD   NA

2. I have ways to handle "bullies"
   in meetings.   SA   A   D   SD   NA

3. I speak up when I have something
   to contribute.   SA   A   D   SD   NA

4. I use a variety of group techniques
   to involve participants.   SA   A   D   SD   NA

VI. Building Relationships

1. I know what I have to offer
   networking contacts.   SA   A   D   SD   NA

2. I use social networking tools
   to connect.   SA   A   D   SD   NA

3. I engage in substance talk vs.
   small talk.   SA   A   D   SD   NA

4. My value is known by others in
   and outside my organization.   SA   A   D   SD   NA

How to Interpret This Quiz:

Review your responses.

There is no numerical scoring of this quiz. The pattern is what is important. Follow these three steps:

1. Circle all responses that fall into the (D) Disagree and (SD) Strongly Disagree categories. Then record four of your responses on the chart in Figure 4. They may cluster in one category or be scattered throughout. Put a sticky note on this page and refer back to it as you read along. By putting the lens on these improvement areas or "soft spots," you can seek specific solutions and be more focused in your use of this book. Of course, you will be learning everything you can to be successful in each leadership area, but pay special attention to these questions you have listed. These are the areas where you will get the most help.

2. Ask for feedback from managers and peers and consider which skills are more valued in your organization to help you

Figure 4. Soft Spots Chart

Strongly Disagree	Disagree

prioritize them. You may find it helpful to ask for your manager's or peers' feedback on how you are doing in these areas.

3. Don't forget your strengths. We spend so much time on fixing what we aren't doing well that we often forget the leadership situations that we already handle well. What are those? Circle all the responses that fall into the Strongly Agree and Agree categories and write at least four of them in the columns in Figure 5.

   How can you build on these assets? For instance, if you do a good job of *sharing the limelight with others* (question III.3), can you bring that strength to another workplace situation? You already do it well, why not capitalize on it and become even more effective? Look for additional examples as you read ahead and learn how others have built upon their pre-existing strengths.

The next six chapters follow the sequence of the quiz. You will be provided with numerous tools that you can apply across the

Figure 5. Strengths Chart

Strongly Agree	Agree

leadership spectrum. In chapter 11, Going Forward, take some time to complete the Developmental Action Plan. You can tie the plan back to this quiz to focus on your next steps. Engage your manager, colleagues, friends, and family members in your efforts. I hope you find these lessons helpful in being the most effective introverted leader you can be.

Let's get started by diving into the first work scenario: public speaking.

Chapter 4

Public Speaking

The year was 2000. It was time to give the annual report to the board, and Suzanne, the vice president of finance, was sweating buckets. The rolls of nausea began before she moved up to the podium. With clammy hands and short breaths, she went through her PowerPoint slides, breathing a sigh of relief when the 20 minutes were up. Fast forward to 2007. A new company and a new board waited. As the A.V. team adjusted her mike, Suzanne came from behind the lectern and watched calmly with a slight smile as the audience members filed in. The paralysis of years ago had disappeared. Under protest, Suzanne had enrolled in a Toastmasters group at her company (push) and attended it consistently for 3 years. She took these learned skills and confidence into her work, seized every opportunity to speak in public (practice), and overcame what could have become a huge career derailer.

Warren Buffet said that public speaking can be our greatest asset or our worst liability.[1] Do you experience what Suzanne felt in her earlier days, or are you able to find your voice and give presentations with ease and confidence? Perhaps you are somewhere in between. We have all heard the statistics about people fearing public speaking more than death. Even the act of getting up and introducing themselves makes introverts in my classes anxious. Their voices and hands shake the first few times they are asked to report out to the group. However, as Warren Buffet said, presenting your ideas coherently in all kinds of situations moves your career forward. Being introverted does not mean you can't also be a phenomenal speaker. Just like an actor goes into character, you can perform brilliantly in your role. As a leader in your organization or profession, you need to educate, inform, and persuade people. You also need to challenge individuals to talk to you and each other. Setting the stage may require laying out a business case or problem to be solved, presenting your ideas, or summarizing results for management. All of these require you to deliver a command performance.

On some level, most people know the steps they need to take to overcome their fear of public speaking. A combination of training and, like the Nike commercial slogan, "just doing it" is part of the formula for success. As the "sales guy, Richard Elmes says, "The presentation you give tomorrow will be that much better because of the speech you delivered today." Life is too short to be paralyzed by this fear. People need to hear what you have to say. Why rob them of that opportunity? Let's look at how you can use the 4 P's model to walk through the steps of becoming a more confident and competent speaker.

Prepare

When I first started as a corporate trainer, I spent days and days preparing for one presentation. I studied the material, tried to anticipate every question, and entered the room ready to be the expert. Of course, I soon realized that though I felt well versed in the material, I could never be totally aware of every fact and every question that might arise. The company had hired a coach to work with our team on presentation skills. He saw my tenseness that day, and before the program, he walked up to the lectern and said, gently, "Jennifer, you know this material. Now enjoy the experience and relax." His words have stuck with me over the years. The synergy of well-prepared material and, even more importantly, your attitude is a winning combination for presentation success.

Prepare the Material
1. Know Your Purpose

You should know the purpose of your program. Is it to inform, persuade, educate, or motivate? Do you know what you want people to leave with? Why should they care about what you have to say? What are the three big points you want to make? Focus in depth on these points, and use lots of examples. Do not overload your audience with numerous points. What do you want them to remember? This will be the basis of your talk. Your preference for introspection will allow you to reflect on this and think it through before putting pen to paper. Being prepared gives you the confidence to get up there and be with your audience. Many introverted professionals I know have said that people do not believe them when they say they are introverts because they look so at ease on the stage. It is the preparation that allows them to relax during the delivery.

2. Tell Me a Story

A few years ago, I heard Montel Williams deliver a keynote speech to a room full of administrative professionals. He told a story about promoting his secretary to president of one of his companies and introduced this woman to the crowd. It was a moving moment, and many of the people in the audience were visibly touched by his showcasing a living, breathing role model. There is power in examples. How many times have you heard a speaker, whether a motivational speaker or your CEO, engage a group by sharing a story? How often have you seen a leader make a point by sharing a personal experience? The use of stories to drive home a point is a skill you too can master.

Stories emphasize ideas a lot more powerfully than bullet points on a slide. The good news is that you can prepare and rehearse these stories to make a much stronger case. This can be done to motivate a team on a project that is lagging, or to influence customers to purchase your product. Today, stories are the key to a successful presentation.

Annette Simmons, a storytelling expert, says, "The human presence in communication is frequently elbowed out by criteria designed to make communication clear, bite sized and attention grabbing, but which instead oversimplifies, truncates and irritates. These 'sub goals' often obscure the real goal: human connection. Communication can't feel genuine without the distinctive personality of a human being to provide context. You need to show up when you communicate. The real you, not the polished, idealized you. The missing ingredient in most failed communication is humanity. This is an easy fix. In order to blend humanity into every communication you send, all you have to do is tell more stories and bingo—you just showed up. Your communication has a human presence."[2]

We are not all natural-born storytellers (coming from someone who forgets the punch line of most jokes!), but you can learn to tell great stories. There are sources of stories all around us: the media, books, movies, television, etc. I think the most powerful stories, however, come from our own experience. This is especially true when we reveal our flaws. It is then that we connect with the audience.

I remember an experience several years ago when our family went whitewater rafting. My spouse, Bill, flipped out of the raft, and because I never really listened to our trusted, pony-tailed guide before the trip, I practically strangled Bill in the process of "rescuing" him. I often use that story (with more graphic details, of course) to make a point about the importance of listening. It certainly wasn't funny at the time, but in retrospect, with time to reflect and weave lessons like that into the story, people can relate to it, and I can make a point at the same time. You can do the same.

Follow a format that works. What is the point you want to make? What was going on in the scene? Include the smells, the sights, and the sounds. You can help the listener be there with you. I am so committed to tell stories in my work now that I keep a small notebook with me and jot down memories and observations. Just open your eyes and you will find stories waiting to be told.

3. No More PowerPoint Karaoke

Though PowerPoint is a great tool, it has become overused and over-relied on by many of us. Too many bullet points on a slide, reading the slide out loud when the audience can do it themselves, and not promoting audience engagement are some negative impacts of PowerPoint. Kevin Smith, a marketing manager at Dell Canada, put it well: "The audience showed up to hear the expert (that's you) talk about a solution to a problem that's causing them pain, not to hear you perform 'PowerPoint karaoke' by reading PowerPoint off of the slides."

Instead, consider using photos, other images, a single question, key words, and even audio to make your points. Cliff Atkinson has some great examples of how to construct these types of presentations on his Web site www.beyondbulletpoints.com. One benefits specialist resisted this approach. I suggested that her audience take notes on an outlined handout, and for her to make the material available online. You are better off providing only the three key points in your presentation on your slides. By writing down the points that are important to them, audience members will increase their retention, and they can get more details in their follow-up online. I don't think people can retain the myriad of benefits details she is providing. Your audiences will appreciate this approach and gain more from your program.

Prepare Yourself

I. Conquer Fear

Fear of public speaking is by no means limited to introverts. The fear that manifests in shaking heads, sweaty palms, and knocking knees is common across the leadership spectrum. Extroverts, because they are more comfortable in conversation, may think they can transfer their conversational skills to the stage. However, speaking to a group calls on different skills. Few people can ad lib when it comes to presentations, nor should they. The introvert's tendency to reflect is a benefit here. Using reflection to tackle the fear will help you be focused and prepared, allowing you to be more spontaneous when you are delivering a program.

To be a confident speaker, you need to get into the right mindset and use the nervous energy you feel. Being in the moment and getting involved with the audience is the key. This is particularly true when reactions come up that you didn't anticipate—and let's face it, you rarely can anticipate reactions. I was speaking at a program a few months ago when I noticed that I wasn't getting much of a reaction. So I decided to move around and get out from behind the lectern. It made all the difference. I was more in my comfort zone, and I think the audience then saw me as a person and not "the speaker." Be open to listening to your gut. This will allow you flexibility.

Scott Mastley, author of *The Confidence Zone* and a professional speaker, told me, "All speakers feel anxious before standing in front of the audience and beginning their talks, but the best speakers focus that nervous energy into a greater level of enthusiasm by reminding themselves of their previous successes, their preparation, and the great feeling that comes from delivering a message of value to people who appreciate it."

2. Visualization

Marny approached me after a class asking for advice. She said that as a pharmaceutical sales rep she has to do many briefings for doctors and other medical personnel. She is an introvert. Recently she had to do a talk in a large lecture hall, and despite the fact that she had learned to manage her nervousness in these smaller briefings, the large venue threw her for a loop. She said it felt scary and awful. What should she do in the future to handle her anxiety?

Visualization is a very powerful technique that I suggested Marny try the next time. Sports heroes such as Tiger Woods use it all the time. Many people tell me they had high school and college coaches who utilized this technique with great results.

Here is how it works. Go to a relaxed, quiet place before the program and imagine a great experience. First, relax your body and get the kinks out. Try listening to calming music on your iPod. Then picture yourself in the room, giving your presentation. Imagine responsive faces, smiles, questions being asked, and your clear compelling answers. The pleasant feeling that you experience in your visualization will last. Your brain essentially is being rewired to experience a calm and positive experience. Visualization is an art. You get better with practice. Some people tell me they are not ever able to visualize. If you are one of these people, don't worry. Not every technique works for everyone, and you can find other ways to calm your nerves, such as taking slow deep breaths.

3. Get Energy

Prepping your mind by pumping yourself up and visualizing success is important. It is also helpful to remember that the whole body needs to be involved. Taking slow, deep breaths prior to speaking relaxes you and helps you to calm mental chatter. A walk or other physical exercise helps you to get the blood going and energy flowing. This can help those with quieter temperaments who may be a little low-key in their presentation. You will feel alert and more alive if you take these steps.

The principles of eating a good breakfast and getting plenty of rest hold true when preparing for speaking. If you are doing a training session, bring healthy snacks that you can nibble on at breaks. Have plenty of water on hand to stay hydrated, and limit caffeine.

4. Rehearse

Practice your talk out loud with a tape recorder. You can also use a video recorder. Listen to how you sound, including the inflections, word emphases, pauses, and timing. It's okay to break your presentation practices into segments. Trying to do the entire presentation at once, and then review the whole thing at once, can get tedious. You will be amazed at how much rehearsing out loud helps. The words on the page will come alive, and you will be more natural when your actual presentation rolls around. By the way, speech coaches also recommend that you tape your program and listen to it afterward to keep improving the delivery, especially if this is a program you will present again.

Rey San Pascuel, a global demand manager, said that his company's communications manager said, "practice, practice, practice," and it made a difference. He said that you could tell who practiced by the smoothness of their delivery. Those who didn't practice fumbled and went over their allotted time.

5. Early, Early, Early

Wendy Kinney, an introverted referral marketing researcher who speaks, told me why she values being early. "I get there early. Really, really, really, really early. I can look over my notes again, or read a magazine, just sit and stare—but I am not stressing about being late or the traffic or the last phone call. And when the meeting planner gets there, they are happy not to worry about me, so they treat me well. I can help them a little (even if it is only to carry a bag), which makes them grateful and friendly and if there is anything about the room that needs to be changed it's no hassle."

Presence

So you have prepared. Now comes the moment to present. Let's consider how to best develop presence on the stage.

In speaking with numerous successful introverts about this, I heard three key themes emerge. They are (1) connect with your audience; (2) use your voice; and (3) use body language

1. Connect with Your Audience

Marilynn Mobley, a senior vice president at Edelman, also coaches people on presentation skills and does media training. She says, "people love to eavesdrop," and advises "looking at one person in the audience because everyone else pays attention to what you are saying to that person . . . so pick a person to lock eyes with as you make an important point, then move to another person, then another, and so on. You'll have great impact, not just on those with whom you lock eyes but with everyone else as well."

Richard Elmes, the sales trainer said, "When I shifted my focus from what I am doing or saying to what the audience is receiving, everything changed. I was less nervous and more effective."

Kathy Armstrong Lee, a communications and community affairs manager, gave a great illustration of how a CFO she saw learned to engage. "He literally couldn't move from behind the lectern—he read his presentation, head down into the microphone. Talk about a rest break—this was a complete snoozer! A year later, with coaching and practice, and a lot of effort at pruning the myriad details from his slides, he was confident enough to use a lavaliere microphone and walk the stage to punctuate his presentation. He described how aspects of what the audience was involved in contributed to the bottom line. He also gave the audience a call to action and a way to focus their efforts. The audience walked out buzzing about how

they finally 'got it' and they were energized by his call to action—
something he never had when just reading financial results."

2. Use Your Voice

Those of you who spend a lot of time on the phone have probably
become adept at "reading" the voices you hear. You can tell if the
person on the other end is rushed, tired, or really on their game. Or
maybe they have learned to pretend.

How we breathe affects how we sound. Renee Grant Williams,
a well-known voice coach, says, "Shallow breathing makes you sound
breathy and weak. Tension around the neck stiffens the vocal chords
making them rigid, unresponsive and vulnerable to damage. It cuts
off the resonance and reduces resilience. . . . You'll get a richer, fuller
voice with a low abdominal breathing because your body and vocal
chords are free to vibrate."[3]

Pausing is one way to use your voice for impact. Introverts are
less afraid of silence than extroverts, so use this to your advantage.
A pause before your point gets your listeners' attention and prepares
them for what is to come. A pause after your point lets the idea sink
in. Renee Grant Williams also says, "Speech is silver, silence is golden
and the power pause is pure platinum."[4] Kevin Horst, a trainer who
speaks, advises "pausing for what may seem to the speaker to be
too many beats after you make a takeaway point, the one you want
the audience to remember and act upon." Use this selectively with
extroverts. One manager told me that her extroverted boss gets visibly impatient if she injects too many pauses. So, remember to flex
to your audience.

Once you are aware that this element of communication can form
up to 85 percent of a person's impression of you, you may decide
to adjust your instrument. You have been asked to brief the boss
about the Galileo project, and the baby got you up at 3:00 A.M. for
a feeding. You want to crawl into bed. Try taking a few full breaths
from your stomach, and slow it down. Watch your energy come back.
You are acting "as if" and will be successful in showing energy and
using your voice more effectively.

3. Use Body Language

The first time I was videotaped doing a training session, I had a flip chart marker in my hand and played catch with it. Hand to hand it went, and I was totally oblivious to the baseball game I was playing. I am sure few eyes and ears were tuned into my pearls of wisdom. They were watching the back-and-forth metronome action.

Wendy Kinney, the referral marketing researcher mentioned earlier, discussed the importance of posture in establishing her stage presence. Like a number of introverted leaders in this book, she said that she chooses who she wants to be that day and "steps into them. So I hold my head the way they would, hold my shoulders the way they would. When I first learned this technique, I often modeled Oprah Winfrey."

Push

Some of the strategies we've talked about in the prepare and presence sections may fall under the push category for you. Here are a few more ideas taken from the mouths of introverts.

Get Serious about Increasing Your Skills

A common recommendation from people who have overcome their fear of speaking in public is, "Join Toastmasters!" Toastmasters (www.toastmasters.com) is a worldwide nonprofit organization with chapters in ninety-two countries. Their mission is to "help people become more competent and comfortable in front of an audience." With weekly opportunities to practice in a nonthreatening atmosphere with constant feedback, you will develop stronger public speaking skills. Of course, you have to keep attending to improve.

Get Creative

A little creativity goes a long way. Look for opportunities to liven up your presentations. I suggested earlier that you consider replacing bullet points on PowerPoint slides with images. I attended a program on humor given by Pat Haley, a former writer for *Seinfeld* who speaks to corporate groups. He shared family photos from the 1960s that had us howling. There are stories in photos that can be shared to make a point and draw the audience in. I still remember the photo of his brothers and sisters at Halloween. He pointed out that his sisters' witch costumes were recycled for the brothers as warlock outfits. You didn't have a choice in his family. Immediately, my mind flashed back on the unusual costumes of my youth and the lack of choice I had, especially the time Mom dressed me as a Russian sputnik space rocket. This kind of connection with your audience will help your presentation have the effect you want. Check out the Web sites online that actually sell the scanned family photos of others. You can also access *New Yorker* magazine cartoons and ask groups to think up their own captions. This solicits some out-of-the-box responses.

My colleague Marty Mercer, a masterful public speaker, told me about a push strategy he used at a recent conference where he spoke. He arrived the night before with his camera in hand. As he wandered around the hotel, he took various shots of attendees. That night Marty downloaded the photos and interspersed them into his slide presentation. He made some humorous comments and had his audience totally engaged and "with him" from the get-go.

Wendy Kinney also pre-plans audience participation. She chooses someone who likes the limelight. She says it is easy to tell who these people are. She listens for their stories and anecdotes and asks for permission to use their example to make her presentations come alive. She might say at lunch, "Oh, I'm going to ask you to share that story. It will come about 15 minutes in, will you do that?" Wendy claims that she feels like a magician who uses diversion, and the audience doesn't see how the trick works.

Practice

You can use tricks to speak with ease, but practice is the magic that will bring out your best. (See Figure 6.) What are the key steps that will move you to public speaking mastery? Speak and speak some more. Take every chance to speak in order to improve and increase your comfort level. How about offering to give a recap of a recent

Figure 6. Public Speaking Practice

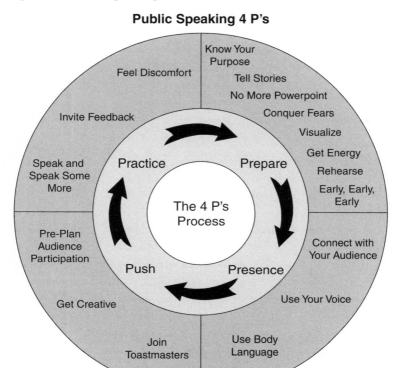

training class at your next staff meeting? What about sharing with the team what you learned about competitive trends in your industry when visiting exhibit booths at a recent conference? Why not tell your boss you are available to present a project status report to the team he usually meets with? Opportunities are all around you to get up and speak. Invite people to observe you and always ask for feedback. Yes, practice is hard and it is uncomfortable, but it is the *only* way to get better.

Chapter 5

Managing and Leading

As a consultant on-site for a few days I could feel the tension. The "suits" were making a visit to the plant, and people seemed on edge. They had heard rumors of corporate changes and, in particular, a shift reduction, meaning fewer overtime opportunities. I watched the vice president of manufacturing walk into the break room. He earnestly approached each individual. I could hear him asking questions, and his attentive body language showed me he was tuned into the answers they were giving. I heard him ask one young worker, "How's your mama?" The man told him about the progress his mother had made since her illness the previous year. These kinds of conversations continued as he made his way around the room.

In the formal update later that day in the cafeteria he gave a sincere picture of the state of the company, and then opened it up to questions. He neither talked down to the group nor appeared to gloss over the challenges ahead. In addition he addressed the overtime issues directly by listening to their concerns and stating his commitment to keep the group informed. When he walked back to his waiting car, I asked several of the workers their impressions and the general consensus was that he "was cool."

This guy had *presence!* He knew an important lesson about getting work done. People want you to treat them as more than cogs in a wheel. They want to matter. By being genuine and showing a sincere interest in people's top-of-mind issues (both personal and work-related), you build trust and honest communication.

Do you remember what it felt like the last time someone asked about your life and your work concerns in a genuine way? When they listened to the answer, you probably felt like you were the only one in the room. This ability to be so truly present with another person is one of the marks of effective leadership.

People who are considered introverted often report that they are more comfortable talking to others in a one-on-one situation than in a group. They are also considered to be excellent listeners who go for depth rather than breadth in their conversations. Often it is a matter of knowing how to begin the conversation. You can start small. Learn people's names. Find out if they have children or pets and use ice-breakers to get the conversation going. The conversation usually will flow when you have hit an interest or concern the other person feels strongly about.

Two caveats: Don't ask so many questions that people feel they are being grilled. Also be sure to truly listen to the answers they are giving you. Many people begin focusing on the next question or person as soon as they finish asking a question. This is something to avoid.

In the beginning, initiating a "how's your mama" dialogue may feel uncomfortable. You may find that the person doesn't want to engage or you are met with silence. That's okay. You are lubricating the wheels of conversation, and some wheels take more oil than others. Be patient. You will see results as you build relationships one conversation and one person at a time.

We will come back to presence in a bit, but first let's look at leadership and introversion. In reviewing a great deal of research on the subject, I have not found specific evidence that says extroverts make better leaders than introverts do. A few studies have looked at introversion specifically, and the research window is open for more exploration on the subject. For instance, one study looked at the fit of city managers.[1] The researchers determined that introverted city managers who were inwardly oriented, reflective, and consider deeply before acting are more likely to have a longer tenure.

A large number of books and articles have been written about the traits of successful leaders. My clients have confirmed that good bosses have some common characteristics similar to the list Daniel Goleman provides in *Social Intelligence*.[2] Good bosses are great listeners, encouragers, communicators, and courageous; they have a sense of humor, show empathy, are decisive, take responsibility, are humble, and share authority.

On the other hand, bad bosses are blank walls, doubters, secretive, and intimidating. They are bad-tempered, self-centered, indecisive, blame others, are arrogant, and show mistrust. Both introverts and extroverts can fit into either of these categories. It may be easier for introverts to exhibit some traits like listening. It may be more natural for extroverts to demonstrate other traits, such as a sense of humor. But all of these traits can surely be mixed and matched. Humor can be just as much a part of the introvert's repertoire of traits as the extroverts. Introvert Warren Buffet was asked what he wanted on his tombstone. With the hint of a smile, he didn't skip a beat and said, "God he was old!"[3]

This chapter is about being a successful leader in an organization. It is drawn from the lessons I have learned from both introverted and extroverted leaders. Let's look at how these suggestions and tools fit into the 4 P's Process.

Prepare

Stepping into a management role is a scary and exciting proposition for most of us. On the one hand, we are usually pleased to have been recognized for our accomplishments. On the other hand, we wonder if we are up to the task. We also are concerned about giving up what we do well to venture into a land of ambiguity.

Stewart Stokes, in an article titled "The Toughest Transition in Information Systems Management" (aimed at mostly introverted types), put it well: "Managing this 'toughest transition' means, first, giving up some of what you know, like to do, and that provides you with a great deal of job satisfaction and self-esteem. Second, it means taking on some of what you do not know, are not sure you will like, and that may not (at least initially) do much for your job satisfaction and self-esteem. Third, it means moving from working on tasks where there is some certainty, specificity, and even some 'answers', and fourth, it means moving to assignments and challenges that may seem vague, unclear, perhaps ill-defined, and worst of all, may appear to lack answers—at least in the short run."[4]

Although no rule book exists for this move, training, coaching, and mentoring will increase your chances of success. You also should consider these steps when making the decision about whether to even move into management at all. It is okay to say no to moving up.

Here are the four touch points to consider in preparation: (1) know yourself; (2) know your team; (3) build in motivation; and (4) see the big picture.

1. Know Yourself

It has been said that the most difficult person you will ever manage is yourself. We have to learn to manage ourselves in order to manage others. How true that is! Knowing yourself means understanding what assets and liabilities you bring to the table. With self-awareness you can learn to use your strengths as a leader and compensate for your weaknesses. In writing our book for human resources professionals, *Shaping Your HR Role: Succeeding in Today's Organizations,* Dr. Bill Kahnweiler and I found that the advantages of knowing yourself are far-reaching.[5] We developed a Career Success Model that identifies six critical self-assessment signposts. They are experience, skills, traits, values, likes and dislikes, and emotional intelligence. When you know your strengths and weaknesses, you can be more objective, detach when you have to, and show appropriate concern for others. Understanding your limitations also allows you to ask for help when you need it, and not shortchange your employees. Self-awareness helps you realize the value you bring to the team and gives you the confidence to ask for the challenging assignments and other opportunities you desire.

Your belief in your own competence will transfer to your employees. In an article about information services leaders as introverts in *Computerworld,* Bob Bolton, a consultant to the Society of Information Management, says, "A leader must have followers. If somebody has a high level of expertise, others will follow that person because of that expertise, not because (that person) can get up on the podium and give a speech."[6]

Blind spots can also emerge. Because you may be comfortable in a hands-on world, for example, you may not let go of tasks soon enough and fail to manage and coach your team, resulting in work overload and missed deadlines. Recognizing lack of delegation as a weakness is something that can be remedied, but only after you take an honest look at yourself through self-assessment activities.

2. Know Your Team

We have touched upon styles in this book. Most people have been exposed to at least one personality instrument by now. The MBTI, or Myers-Briggs Type Indicator, in addition to high lighting introvesion and extroversion, describes other dimensions of personality, such as Sensing, Intuition, Thinking, and Feeling. Knowing these preferences makes a tremendous difference in how you adapt your approach to people.

You should plan on how to approach people in the preparation stage. For instance, let's say you want to get your team on board with a big project. Your employee who is very high on the Sensing scale will be focused on facts and details. Another employee may be a strong Intuitor who will be listening for the big picture from you. If you know these subtle differences about these teammates, you will increase your chances of getting them committed much faster. Prepare in advance by getting a handle on the styles, skill sets, and other preferences of those you will be supervising. You may already have insights into this if you have been promoted from within the group.

Chuck Papageorgiou, managing partner of Ideasphere Partners, LLC, is a long-time colleague and successful entrepreneur who has always impressed me with his ability to adapt his style. I asked him about the leadership approach he uses with introverts. Chuck, an extroverted manager, finds that when he "creates the right environment, there is no difference in performance between extrovert and introvert managers/executives." He does change his style somewhat with introverts, however. He will, when faced with a challenge, "spend a few minutes creating a short but very clear request or description of the problem, present it to those managers with a timeframe for a solution, and then walk away." Chuck allows the more introverted managers on his team to internalize the challenge, process the information, and get him an answer without feeling they have to come up with a response on the spot. Interestingly, he also told me that he will use that approach successfully with extroverted managers "so they don't give me the first answer that comes to their minds."

3. Build in Motivation

Is it possible to prepare to motivate your employees? Yes. Part of the process involves understanding what motivates your people. Each person is different. Meeting with people one-on-one in the first 90 days of your job is a great strategy to understand more about who they are. You can then adapt your approach to match their needs. One IT manager I know realized that giving his top performer a vacation day was not an effective reward, but assigning him a complex problem to solve with time to focus on it really juiced him up.

Bob Quinn is an introverted HR manager who believes that people are motivated by the manager showing true respect and inclusion. Even though he it is not a natural extrovert, he has made walking around and talking with people each day a part of his motivational preparation. When Bob was in charge of a merger, he personally met with each affected person and listened to their concerns. He then met with his top managers and designed the integrated team from scratch. Bob said, "By the day of the merger, everyone knew exactly what they would be doing." He also arranged for brunches to take place in each office, gave each new associate a bottle of wine, and appointed a buddy to help the newly integrated employees understand the culture. He reported that he received some of the nicest thank-you notes that he has ever received from the people who chose to package out. He knew things were going well, he said, when one of the mid-level managers looked at him and said, "You're not so bad."

Bob Schack, a vice president of business development, has a background in leadership positions at companies like Cisco Systems and Northern Telecom. Bob, a professed extrovert, has always led groups of very bright, highly technical people. He knows that team members are motivated differently and have varying levels of risk tolerance. Despite that, he also believes that you can motivate a team by getting them all engaged and involved in the outcome of the project. At one point, he and several others moved on to other companies, but because the excitement about a certain project was so high, they continued to work on this project through their new organizations. He even said that he will meet with these same people 10 years later because "we have formed a personal bond." That is motivation!

Management consultant and author Marcus Buckingham believes that motivating employees is best done on a case-by-case basis. He writes that great managers know how to play the game of chess, rather than checkers. They learn how each chess piece moves and then incorporate these moves into their plan of attack.[7]

4. See the Big Picture

Stepping into management shoes means that you need to tap into the right side of the brain. Stewart L. Stokes, in talking to IT managers, said, "The left side of the brain—the side that many IT professionals prefer and find most comfortable—is our analytical, structured, predictable and orderly side. The left side is where managers like to live and leaders often feel uncomfortable. The right side of the brain is where leaders like to live and managers often feel uncomfortable. It is our more unstructured, experimental, creative, visionary and less orderly side. We manage from the left and we lead from the right. The sides are different but complementary. Certainly both are needed but increasingly, as you get away from the hands on, tactical work you need to create a vision, connect your department's work to the organization and step back and see how you can creatively apply your resources (human and other)." [8]

Daniel Pink believes that leaders need to move away from the notion of focus. Just as a composer and conductor know that parts of orchestras need to play together, it is the entire orchestra that sounds magnificent. Symphony is the ability to grasp the relationship between relationships. Pink believes that it is a vital skill for the conceptual age in which we live. He told me how he thought his notion of symphony might connect with the introvert. "Symphony is important to all leaders—but quiet leaders might have an edge because they do more listening—and therefore might get more and better information."[9]

One practical suggestion Pink makes is to "turn your bulletin board into an inspiration board. Each time you see something compelling—a photo perhaps, or the page of a magazine—pin it to the board. Before long, you'll start seeing connections between the images that will enliven and expand your thinking." Prepare for your leadership role by using your right brain's powers as well as your left brain's, and the results will be powerful.

Presence

Making a profound impression on people is one aspect of presence. I attended a convention where the keynote speaker, William Strickland Jr., mesmerized the crowd. Bill is an inspirational leader who has devoted his life and work to the poor youth of Pittsburgh. He has received international recognition and has replicated the best practices from his art and job training centers across the country. In the speech I heard, his message and delivery were so compelling that tears and sniffles were seen and heard throughout. Bill spoke from the heart. After his speech I took a break, only to stumble upon him surrounded by a small group of people. Someone whispered, "It is like being in the presence of the Pope!" I had to agree. There was a feeling of reverence that permeated the air around this humble man. I found myself face to face with Bill as he handed me his card and said, "Please come visit our center in Pittsburgh." His eyes connected with mine. Whether he pressed his business card and made that invitation to everyone in that small crowd did not matter. For those few seconds, I had his sincere attention. I am sure that Bill's sincerity and intensity reached the CEOs such as the late John Heinz and Jeff Bezos, founder of Amazon, who became some of his many corporate sponsors. That is presence.

The next sections will explore three elements of presence that I have observed in successful leaders: (1) learn to delegate; (2) listen with attunement; and (3) observe facial expressions.

1. Learn to Delegate

In management classes I have led over the years, delegation seems the hardest skill for new managers to master. Yet it is probably the most needed. How can you ever lead, plan, and coach if you are holding onto the many tactical aspects of your job? One company I know offers a "delegation boot camp" in response to this need. Learning how to delegate is not the hard part. It is a matter of matching the right person to the right task, knowing the capabilities of that person, and coaching them. If you can guide them more in the beginning and then slack off as they gain mastery, delegation can be successful.

The greatest barrier that I see, however, to embracing delegation is under the surface. Each of us has hot buttons that keep us from handing over the keys. I have experienced them all as a manager, until I learned that this resistance was holding me back from embracing leadership. If you are honest with yourself in the preparation phase, then you can identify your potential barriers to letting go of tactical work. What are your delegation hot buttons? Consider the counterarguments for each of them in Figure 7 to overcome your barriers.

Figure 7. Delegation Hot Buttons

Why Not to Delegate	Your Counterargument
I don't want to take the time to train someone else.	This is an investment with great potential payoffs. The rewards of building confidence in your employees and freeing time for you to focus on what matters is worth the training time.
They won't do it the way I do.	Yes—and it may be better or just different. The results are what matter.
I am still the one responsible for the results.	Yes—and you can also share the positive kudos with your team for a job well done.
Add your own delegation hot button here: _____ _____	Add your counterargument here: _____ _____

Bruce, an introverted friend, recently shared an example of how he had gained respect for his boss at a trade show they both attended. Bruce is a laid-back software designer who was staffing their booth in the exhibit area. His job was to chat up visitors to the booth and then turn them over to his boss to take follow-up action. His first few attempts were dismal failures. The conversation stopped after some initial chit-chat, and the potential customers moved on to other booths. His boss then made a wise, in-the-moment decision. He switched positions and became the greeter, bringing his "catches" back to Bruce, who then answered any and all technical questions. By making this move on the fly, Bruce's boss saved the situation and gathered some potential prospects. Bruce felt that his talents were being used to help the company, and it was an overall win-win solution.

2. Listen with Attunement

The vice president of manufacturing introduced in the beginning of chapter 5 showed adeptness in listening. Attunement is the term that Daniel Goleman uses for this type of listening skill. He describes this as "attention that goes beyond momentary empathy to fully, sustained presence that facilitates rapport. . . . We can all facilitate attunement simply by intentionally paying more attention." Goleman says that real listening means we have a back-and-forth dialogue and "we allow the conversation to follow a course we mutually determine." This kind of deep listening, he argues, is what distinguishes the best managers.[10] I like his term of having an "agenda less" presence. You aren't there to make the sale or prove your point, but to listen, or, as Steven Covey said, "seek first to understand."[11] It takes more focus than time to really listen. When Bill Strickland tuned in to me, it was for less than a minute. But his sharp focus was undeniable. For the busy manager, this means looking up from your laptop or Blackberry. It may even mean scheduling some time with your employees when you can totally focus. It is your behavior, not your intention, that people will remember when it comes to listening.

It is commonly thought that introverts are better listeners. John Pietruszkiewicz, an introverted professional engineer, reinforces this point. John says that introverted people are more contemplative and better listeners. "You don't learn by speaking," he says, "you learn by listening." He also believes that many extroverts don't communicate well because they don't take time to listen. John, like most people I have come across, believes that this skill can be developed. Kevin Horst, the introverted trainer you met in chapter 4 who effectively uses silence in his presentations, applies this same technique in his leadership role at work. He said that most of the time he simply listens to his team's ideas and suggestions after he has shared the goal and timeframe. If they are too far off base, he may use silence. Kevin says his team knows him well enough at this point to understand that he is looking for more or different approaches.

Stephen Bigelow, a director of operations, maintains flexibility in his listening style, but often uses techniques similar to that described by Kevin. He lays out organizational goals, objectives, and tasks on the table, then lets his team work it out. This has worked well for him, he said. He, like most effective leaders I have observed, adapts his style depending on the people and situation. "It requires me to step outside of my comfort zone." Kevin also said that he steps out of his normal listening mode when surrounded by extroverts or a group of pure introverts. With the extroverts, he steps up his engagement and active listening.

Interestingly, not everyone believes that introverts are naturally better listeners. Scott Byorum, an introverted director of business development, doesn't think that being an introvert causes you to be a naturally good listener. Scott thinks that "people express themselves and open up to introverts because introverts are less likely to challenge them negatively or criticize them." He thinks that if an introvert can "harness the power of listening with assertiveness, it can position them into an ideal manager/leader type. I am generally reserved and quiet. People open up to me without hesitation. I am able to gather info easily with relatively few pointed questions, analyze it, and articulate a direction at the opportune time. . . . I think with introspection comes a heightened sense of observation."

3. Observe Facial Expressions

A joke: How do you tell an extrovert in the IT department? He is the one looking at your shoes instead of his own! Admittedly, even extroverts have some work to do in the area of presence. We all can smile more.

Hokey, you say? Consider the story of Nelson Mandela, the great South African leader. Apparently, he was a pretty dull speaker. What he did consistently in every setting was break out his huge smile. This symbolized his lack of bitterness toward white South Africans and communicated hope and triumph to black voters. Mandela's smile was his message.[12]

Aren't you drawn to those leaders with smiles? Sometimes in tough yoga poses, when I am straining in both a mental and physical way, a wise teacher will put out the suggestion to smile. In a strange way, the act of moving those facial muscles seems to make the pose easier. I don't worry about the past or future; I stay in the present.

I was in a meeting the other day with a woman I admire. She is bright, insightful, and always pulls her weight. Unfortunately, in that meeting, if looks could kill, she was committing murder. She sat there with a flat expression on her face the entire time. Smiling at appropriate times, such as when she met someone's eye, would be a way for her to change the perception that she is unapproachable.

In addition to being aware of projecting a friendly image yourself, it can be a great advantage to become adept at reading faces. Since Malcolm Gladwell's book *Blink*[13] was published there has been more interest in the concept of micro expressions. He actually popularized the ideas of researcher Paul Ekman, whose book *Emotions Revealed* helps the reader learn to recognize subtle facial expressions. According to Ekman, even though we may have the innate ability to read these expressions, we need a little help in interpreting them.[14]

For introverts, becoming more competent at demonstrating your emotions and reading others' facial expressions may be a way to close the perception gaps, reduce stress, and be present.

Ekman's revealing test, which you can take before and after you read the book, demonstrates that you can get better at reading people by learning to interpret these partial or slight expressions. He even found that people across different cultures agreed on facial expressions. The author Daniel Pink believes that everyone should have a copy of Ekman's book to navigate the world of business.

Leaders working with culturally diverse groups need to have the ability to read facial expressions. If you see a person smiling and you think they are not happy, you can probe or observe to better understand what is really going on. For example, last year in Europe I found myself with a group that was used to a more formal method of presentation than I was providing. They were pretty stone-faced. As we developed a rapport, I noticed their faces relax, along with their bodies. I clued into their eyes and consciously read that their responsiveness was increasing.

In summary, you can establish presence by delegating, listening with attunement, and observing facial expressions. These key strategies will set you up to add push approaches that can move you even further toward high performance as a leader.

Push

These push techniques also incorporate preparation and presence approaches. As a newly emerging leader, don't try to change everything overnight. Review your assessment in chapter 3 to see what else you can incorporate into your leadership plan. This section lists some push strategies to incorporate into your plan: (1) assert yourself; (2) have conversations; (3) face conflict; (4) learn about the organization; and (5) keep learning. Let's look at each one of them.

1. Assert Yourself

Assertiveness is often confused with aggressiveness. It is *not* bullying. It *is* direct, open, and honest communication. My daughter, Jessie, who has served in many waitress positions, told me what is done with the food of those patrons who act aggressively in their demands! On the other end of the spectrum, restaurants miss out when customers are unassertive in giving direct feedback. Patrons don't get to have a satisfying meal, and the restaurant does not get to improve their service.

Many new managers fall victim to their own lack of assertiveness in an effort to please others or avoid conflict. Unfortunately, resentment and frustration can build up, resulting in passive-aggressive behavior. At work, these folks get the reputation as "that jerk," or as the boss from hell. Tammy, one such leader, couldn't hold on to her people. She didn't say much, but when she did, her words were sarcastic and ugly, which lead to high turnover in her group.

Asking for what you need in a direct, open, and honest manner is recommended in life and at work. Sid Milstein, when an executive at GE, had the mandate of implementing Six Sigma throughout the business in an initial climate of resistance. When he shared information he was clear and direct, and everyone understood their next steps. When there were questions, he was open to dialogue.

Learn to be assertive by watching those leaders who communicate assertively. It is a process that can be practiced in venues outside of work. Take classes, watch role models, and hone this skill. The benefits will be great for everyone in your life.

2. Have Conversations

There was a theory back in the eighties called MBWA, which stands for management by walking around. The idea was to encourage managers to get out of their offices and talk to people. Revolutionary for the time, it is commonly accepted today. But with so many more complex distractions, it is not always followed even though it is important. Make time, even if you have to schedule it, to talk to the people who work with you.

Emily, an introverted customer service manager, expressed dismay that since being promoted to manager she rarely left her office. She said, "The temptation is to get your reports written and handle communication electronically." My clients who have the strongest relationship with their managers talk with them at least weekly. These interactions are usually project updates, but they also can include "how's your mama" conversations.

One former boss of mine used a conversational aid that combined the steps of presence and preparation. Jon carried index cards around with the name of each direct report at the top of each card.

As he went through the week, he wrote down feedback, specific questions, and new ideas he had. He would stop in with each of us at intervals, and use his list as his agenda. We all kidded Jon about being anal, but the truth was that we were interested in knowing what he had written on our card that week! In addition to being prepared and a very efficient use of time, Jon made each of us feel recognized (presence).

One program manager I interviewed recommended recording the names of people you compliment and whose performance you reinforced, and to note the frequency of such feedback. Because what is measured is often what gets done, you will find this increasing the rate of your positive feedback. If you cringe at the idea of spontaneous, face-to-face, impromptu meetings, using these approaches should help you feel more prepared as you enter the presence and push steps of this action.

3. Face Conflict

Conflict is any disagreement between people. Though the definition by itself is not negative, many of us experience discomfort when team members disagree, employees push back, or bosses question us. It helps to remember that conflict is *natural, necessary, and normal.* In fact, creative solutions to problems rarely occur without the tension of dissimilar ideas.

As he excitedly explained to me, Bob Schack, the vice president of business development introduced earlier, is not afraid of conflict. He said there can be "a lot of egos and opinions at play." Bob actually creates "a firestorm" by drafting a "straw man" plan. He shoots it out to his team via e-mail knowing that he is going to generate all kinds of momentum and discussion. After a lot of back-and-forth discussion, what emerges is consensus and action. You can also use conflict as the lever for productive action. Orchestrate a productive process of dialogue to engage both the introverts and extroverts on your team.

Managing conflict constructively is a challenge. It is also a necessary competency for managers. Not only will you be managing people from many different cultural and ethnic backgrounds, but you may already be working across the globe with customers, vendors, and partners. One introverted Dutch manager told me that her team in the U.S. is more sensitive to direct feedback, but her employees in Holland expect ongoing constructive comments from her. Therefore she has to adjust her approach with each group to be effective. As a leader, the more educated you can become in learning ways to move through these issues, the more ahead of the game you will be.

4. Get Organizational Knowledge

Branch out of your specialty area and learn more about your organization and industry. Like the symphony or big picture we discussed earlier, learn to connect the work of your group to the vision of the organization. Be up on trends so you can suggest directions for upper management to explore. In this knowledge economy, you add value by the ideas you bring.

Develop high organizational acumen. Spend time in the field and take temporary assignments in other areas of the organization. This all contributes to a much deeper understanding and insight into how you are connected to your organization, and you will also gain more visibility. As a result you will be able to translate the bigger vision to your team. Yes, it may be a huge step outside your comfort zone, but it's one you won't regret.

Learn to think in terms of results that matter to your company. It may be cost savings or increased revenues. What are the bottom-line benefits that matter? Education, government, and nonprofit organizations have different measures of success that are important to them. Is it higher enrollments or grant monies that you obtain? Whether selling up or down the organization, learn about what really matters to all your customers.

Practice

Figure 8 is a summary of the steps you can take to practice strengthening your leadership muscle. Refer back to it often.

Surround yourself with a support system. Even though you value your time alone, you can schedule one-on-ones and communicate in writing with these members of your informal advisory board. No

Figure 8. Managing and Leading Practice

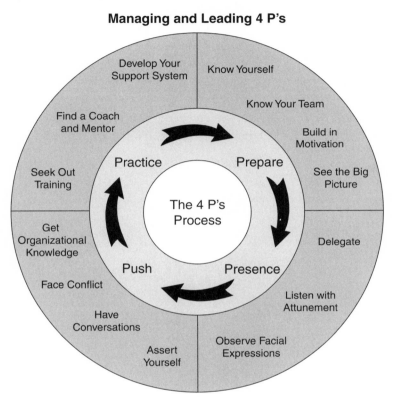

Managing and Leading 4 P's

one succeeds by themselves. You can hire a coach, enlist a mentor, and rely on experienced team members. One introverted woman I know put off a discussion with an employee to avoid conflict. She gritted her teeth and sent a quick e-mail to her coach which prepared her for a discussion that ended up going very well. Another practice strategy is to ask for the training you need to be successful. Enrolling in both classroom and online seminars can be a way to help you practice these skills and gather a wide variety of differing and helpful views from other participants.

Becoming a manager is not for everyone. One introverted vice president of human resources shared, "I was never totally comfortable with the management role and always preferred being an individual contributor. But I overcame my discomfort to respond to the call of duty! I convinced myself that these were opportunities for personal and professional development. Ugh!"

I hope he feels like it was worth the sacrifices he made. You need to decide whether you want to take that step. You may find that you have a hidden talent to inspire others. Or you may find that managing and leading take too much energy and the risk is not worth the reward. But keep in mind that being an introvert is no reason to avoid this step.

Chapter 6

Heading Up Projects

Danielle, an experienced and reserved civil engineer, received a call from her manager asking her to check on the progress of a job across town. As one of the few females in the company, she had learned to step out of her shell, and she usually received respect from the guys. They joked together, talked shop, and generally seemed at ease. Danielle pulled up to the construction site in her pickup truck and asked Bob, the foreman, to come grab a cup of coffee with her. As they rode down the highway, he told her about problems with a sub-contractor who had not lived up to their on-time commitment for supplies. Together Danielle and Bob formulated a plan to make the supplier accountable. When she dropped Bob off at his work station 30 minutes later they were both committed to see the plan work.

Maybe it wasn't in a pickup truck, but have you ever had a productive work conversation in an informal setting? If so, you probably found that it made it easier for you and the other person to open up. In a relaxed atmosphere you can ask questions and get input without being threatening. Finding out about what is going on from those you are leading or influencing is essential so that you can engage in productive solutions and move on. The heart of project management is being able to influence people who often don't report to you and to get results. Managing your perception as a strong leader often takes a willingness to meet people on their turf and step out of the confines of your world.

Prepare

Project management (see Figure 9) is also the main way work gets done. It emerged from the information technology field and now marketing, finance, and human resources all talk in project terms. Projects

Figure 9. Project Management Skills

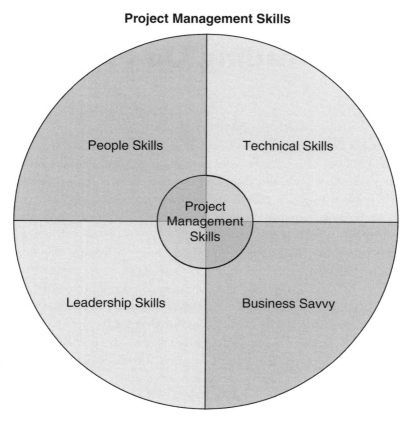

involve the efforts of people across several functions. Project management certification typically includes training in people skills, leadership skills, technical skills, and business savvy.[1] This is further evidence that planning for interpersonal interactions is as important as understanding obviously concrete areas such as cost and scope management. We will focus on some of the people and leadership skills of project management that are necessary for introverted project managers to succeed.

As you prepare to step up to project management leadership, here are three success strategies to consider: (1) coach and mentor; (2) build credibility; and (3) communicate expectations.

1. Coach and Mentor

Jane, a coaching client, said her introverted project manager played a significant role in getting her visibility on a recent project. The project manager first encouraged Jane by meeting with her and reviewing documents before meetings (preparation) to analyze the implications. She then coached Jane on what individual team members wanted and appropriate questions to ask. Jane felt this pre-work emboldened her, and as a result of this coaching she contributed to the project more fully.

Alex Brown, project management professional (PMP), believes that project managers need to mentor team members. In some organizations, department managers have responsibility for career development and advice, leaving the project managers in charge of only project issues. To build a solid project team, though, Brown believes a project manager must diffuse difficult personnel conflicts and identify skills development needs within the team. These activities require negotiating and mentoring.

2. Build Credibility

Mark, a soft-spoken information technology project manager who attended one of my seminars, worked for a large accounting firm. He was faced with a dilemma. Only 50 percent of the invitees showed up at the last three meetings he had scheduled. This was unacceptable because these people had to be there to make decisions, and the project was behind schedule because of these missing links. I learned that Mark had not talked to the team members individually at the outset of the project, and neglected to tell them how and why their involvement mattered. He also had not discussed the benefits of the project to them, their departments, and the organization as a whole. I suggested that he try to repair the damage by scheduling individual meetings first, to find out more about why they were ditching meetings (prepare). He had little chance of influencing them without better understanding their needs and priorities. By talking with them after laying this groundwork (push), he will be able to uncover the needs and concerns of his stakeholders. What are the roots of their concerns? Mark's preference as an introvert to have one-on-one conversations with people

Figure 10. Stakeholder Analysis Chart

	1	2	3	4	5
Shane					
Char					
Joe					
Mary					
Susan					

and really listen lends itself well to this fact-finding process. Perhaps he has to schedule the meetings at a different time, or maybe a project member's boss needs some convincing. But it is apparent he needs to ask questions before he can gain commitment.

I suggested Mark do a stakeholder analysis. A sample chart is shown in Figure 10. Credibility is rated from 1, low commitment, to 5, high commitment.

He can plot his current level of credibility with each of his project stakeholders. These are the people he needs in order to be successful on this project. He could determine where he needs them to be (strongly on board, medium, or not important), then plan how to strengthen his credibility. He can decide how much effort he needs to put into persuading each member to participate and what his approach might be with each one. Shane may just need an e-mail outlining the benefits of the project, whereas Char may need a business case and formal presentation. This approach will probably allow him to plan his strategy and prevent further problems.

3. Communicate Expectations

I participated in a volunteer project that was mishandled in a number of ways. Though the overall vision was laid out, ownership of tasks was murky, few checkpoints were built in, and roles and responsibilities took twists and turns. It left the team demotivated and frustrated, and the project outcomes were disappointing.

I have also been on projects where the effective use of time and resources resulted in success. My clients and colleagues who manage projects for a living say that outlining clear expectations is the key. They suggest you ask, what is the end goal? How will you measure whether outcomes have been achieved?

Erika Flora, PMP and program manager at NexBio said, "If you expect weekly status reports, let people know that when you are planning the project. Otherwise, it becomes next to impossible to hold people accountable. In addition, clearly outline roles and responsibilities and tell people exactly when things are due. It takes the ambiguity out of who needs to be doing what and by when. As an introvert, it takes a lot of the fear and pressure off of me and the team in having to follow up on tasks later on."

Written forms of communication also minimize the need for lots of verbal explanation up front. I spoke with an introverted administrator at a nonprofit agency who has devised a useful form to communicate with her project team. She created a sheet that lists the name of the project, target completion date, task list, participants, tasks, and due dates for each person. She sends it to each person for reactions and edits, and also is sure to include "words of appreciation and encouragement" in her written communication. In addition she makes herself accessible as the project proceeds if people have questions and encounter roadblocks.

Presence

Even though the discipline of managing projects incorporates planning and therefore focused alone time is necessary, it is also necessary to meet with people. The sponsor of the project, team members, and any other stakeholders that are impacted should all be included in this communication. This is how you manage risks.

Successful technical professionals and other successful introverted project leaders learn to segue between the extroverted and introverted sides of their personalities in order to meet the demands of this multifaceted project management role. They seem to thrive on the chance to solve problems, and they don't shy away from communicating in person. In fact, they learn how important it is to engage with people in order to get results.

Exhibiting the quality of presence in project management can be categorized in three key ways.: (1) solicit input; (2) match the medium to the message; and (3) learn to flip the switch.

1. Solicit Input

As an introverted project manager, Erika Flora always includes the perspectives of the more withdrawn members in the group. She believes that otherwise she misses out on many great ideas. As an example, she goes around the room calling people by name to ask for their views. She says that people need to feel that their opinions count.

C.J. Dorgeloh, an experienced and introverted project manager, said, "I generally have to push myself to bring a presence of leadership to public and group situations. I am much more comfortable behind the scenes. As a project leader, there are definite times when . . . I can be very quiet taking it all in. This can hamper my effectiveness as a leader if I'm not aware of addressing it. The group may view this as confusion or lack of direction [perception gap] so I need to consciously verbalize more often than I would naturally to keep them in the loop and things moving."

2. Match the Medium to the Message

While writing this book, I received a query from a reporter who was doing a story about people who have been fired by e-mail. Apparently there are a large number of people who have received the ax through opening an e-mail. Most of us would probably agree that at the very least a phone conversation would be the most appropriate medium for such a situation.

E-mail is effective for relaying information such as appointments and data. Reports to be read, business cases, and plans all fit well into this format. Text messages and instant messages are great for quick answers and for on-the-spot planning around logistics.

The phone is best when you want to reinforce an e-mail you have sent. It can also be useful to connect by phone when you want to develop a relationship and build credibility. Your voice and tone can convey positive reinforcement more personally than an e-mail can. I received a voicemail from Jared, a client who asked me to call him directly. When I reached him, Jared explained a sensitive client situation to me that I probably would have misunderstood if he had described it in an e-mail. Jared's credibility immediately rose because he had taken the time to consider my reaction.

Face-to-face communication is the preferred format to deliver important news, such as being fired in the above example, launching a project, giving praise to the team, or working out issues and problems (see chapter 8, The Meeting Game). This type of communication is also effective when giving clear and specific improvement feedback because you are able to ask and answer questions. Of course, when separated by distance, the phone will have to do. Consider webcam technology as a way to bridge the gap in long-distance working relationships. More people are using Skype and videoconferencing. You should also schedule at least one face-to-face visit if you can fit the travel into your budget. Don't underestimate the impact of even occasional live conversations.

Being selective about when it is necessary to have spontaneous in-person dialogue is important for introverted project managers. Too much interaction becomes exhausting for introverts. Consider the "stop and chat." On several episodes of *Curb Your Enthusiasm*,[2] Larry David laments the situation where you run into someone and are compelled to talk. Most introverts seem to disdain this superficial chatter, so decide when it is important to do this and when you can avoid putting introverted team members in this situation. If you are introverted, watch the people around you and see if you can moderate your behavior to bring some occasional "stop and chats" into your daily schedule.

There has been other pushback against talking in various blog posts. In his highly trafficked piece titled *Passing as an Extrovert*,[3] blogger Shannon Kalvar wrote about this type of communication in the world of project management. He said, "Get out of the front lines. We are introverts, not extroverts. It's not necessary for us to speak with everyone, all the time, and everyday." His suggestion? "Find an extrovert on the team." He says a "kind of front-office/back-office approach to project management (whether done with a team leader or two project managers) can produce impressive results. Good luck, my fellow introverts, and remember: it is no longer considered ok to growl at the person who comes into your cube for the fifteenth time that day to discuss his potted plants."[3]

3. Learn to Flip the Switch

Project performance has a direct connection to the personality composition of team members. In some interesting research done with ninety-two information services professionals on twenty software teams in Hong Kong, team members were asked to provide their perceptions of team performance. One dimension of several that were considered was whether the individual was an introvert or extrovert. The researchers found that a team was higher performing when there was a difference in the personality dimension between its team leader and team members.[4] This dimension was more important than the differences between team members.

So what does this mean? Quite possibly, knowing team members' style preferences can help the insightful team leader to assign appropriate work and motivate people according to their preferences. They can also choose people with styles that complement their own.

Part of the challenge and opportunity for the project manager is that they must continually call on many facets of their style in leading teams. They literally must "flip the switch" when working with extroverts vs. introverts. They must rely on personal influence vs. their position (my authority will make you perform) to get results. One project manager, Donna Fitzgerald, shared the following:

> By understanding the difference between Extroverts and Introverts, the nimble project manager is freed from having to push a one-size-fits-all solution on the project team. Functional teams (usually a group of extroverts) can schedule as many meetings as they want or need to think out loud, while the

development team members can sit in their cubes, collaborating when they need to through Web-based discussion threads. Meetings where both groups need to be present (status meetings, etc.) can then be conducted with a middle-ground goal in mind. Less frequency or shorter durations and clearly defined agendas actually tend to keep both groups happy.

C.J. Dorgeloh, the project manager mentioned earlier, manages the extroverts by limiting reports. She also has learned to assign the extroverts to "the big social situations and schmoozing responsibilities. They naturally take up more space and are a little more visual and vocal in their participation," so she uses participatory meeting tools to achieve more balance. C.J. said that being an introvert brings great value to the processes of negotiating and getting buy-in from teams and partners. "I work very well in one-on-one conversations, giving people a feeling of being heard and listened to and creating a sense of trust in the relationship. I am not easily distracted or prone to multitask, so I bring a focus to my conversations and interactions which I have been told feels good. . . . My extroverted counterparts can look very busy and productive with all of their externally driven multi-tasking." The introverted nonprofit project manager mentioned earlier added that she tries to appreciate the extroverts' strengths "out loud." She sometimes has to ask them to quiet down and limit their chatting, but doesn't try to "fuss too much about that," because the same trait is also a positive for the department. She encourages the introverts to speak to her one-on-one and ask questions. Checking in with each person on her team (introverts and extroverts) each day makes a big difference.

Push

I have always admired successful project managers. They communicate in terms that are clear to nontechnical people. They seem to be excellent liaisons with people across and outside the organization. The technical project managers would probably agree with authors Gorla and Lam, who wrote about project management in their field, "It appears that the human aspects of software development are more important than the technological aspects for better performance."[5]

They have pushed themselves to excel outside their comfort zones. So what are some of the additional qualities that set these leaders apart? What lessons can introverted project leaders take to push their own performance forward? Here are three push strategies to consider: (1) share the limelight; (2) deal with change; and (3) appreciate the value of humor.

1. Share the Limelight

As an emerging or current project manager, you can look for opportunities to praise the team as milestones are reached. It is common in some company cultures to have celebrations with food such as cake or pizza. It also can be helpful to use the communication tools of your company such as the intranet and newsletters to update the organization on milestones that have been reached. One project manager told me that she makes a "big deal when we are ahead of plan."

It is particularly important to recognize individual contributions as well. This is motivating to people, and, on a more practical level, leads to future raises and promotions. Chester Elton, author of *The Carrot Principle,* said, "Employees who feel valued and appreciated are much more likely to be fully engaged and to clearly contribute to the success of the business."[6]

Keep in mind that not all team members want to receive their kudos in the same way. I have worked with some team members who relished a special verbal commendation at staff meetings. One researcher I partnered with did not want public recognition, but did want me to send an e-mail to his boss and the senior leaders on his team. Knowing people's preferences for rewards is very helpful. Remember your team members, but don't forget to recognize yourself and take needed breaks to refresh and recharge.

Another way to share the limelight is to continually update project stakeholders as the project unfolds. This will demonstrate your competence. Your desire to keep key people informed will help to close the perception gap that occurs when you are out of sight and out of mind. So while you lead your team in a quiet and steady way, also be sure to be visible.

2. Deal with Change

Today, managing projects occurs against a backdrop of changing business conditions. Aaron Shenhar, co-author of *Reinventing Project Management*, said that "there are still projects that are very much predictable. But most projects are created in a very uncertain world . . . in any project you cannot—I emphasize, you cannot— plan everything in advance because so many changes happen."[7]

What does this mean for you as a person who manages projects as part of your job? We have already said that you must communicate *often and clearly* with team members and all stakeholders. Asking questions, listening to concerns, and translating new directions become key parts of your role. For an introvert, this constant and consistent communication can be a stretch.

Some of the push strategies in chapter 4, Public Speaking, can help you raise your comfort level in communicating and getting your message across. This is especially important in a climate of change. People feel unsettled and look to their leaders for information and reassurance during times of uncertainty. As an introvert, your calm focus and careful preparation will help people. To increase the "stickiness" of your message liven up your presentations with creative approaches such as photos and storytelling. This is a push step. For instance, I spoke with Martin Schmidler, the introverted vice president of information technology, after he took a storytelling class. He was pleased with the success he had in incorporating stories into his team meetings, particularly when making a case for upcoming company changes.

Initiate meetings with the boss. Another push tactic during change is to continually strengthen your relationships. You will learn more about the current and future picture in your company and how it may affect your department. A former boss of mine did this very well, and switched the course of our team in time to save our jobs and get us working on what turned out to be mission critical for the company.

3. Appreciate the Value of Humor

Victor Borge said, "A smile is the shortest distance between two people." As a quieter team leader, you can overcome the perception that you are overly serious and that only the "talkers" can laugh. You need your ideas heard to gain cooperation. Use laughter and show the side of you that can have some fun.

More organizations are recognizing the significance of what Daniel Pink in his book *A Whole New Mind*[8] calls "play." Pink states that games, humor, and joyfulness are finding a rightful place in our new "Conceptual Age." He goes on to say that "humor can be a cohesive force in organizations, as anyone who's ever traded jokes at the water cooler or laughed over lunch with colleagues understands." Pink quotes a study by Fabio Sala, published in *Harvard Business Review,* that indicates that "humor used skillfully greases the management wheels."[9] "According to this research," writes Pink, "the most effective executives deployed humor twice as often as middle-the-pack-managers." There seems to be a connection between humor and high emotional intelligence.

What does this mean for the quieter leader? People are following your lead. When you show you can laugh, you and the team enjoy several benefits. (1) The team sees that you are more than all about the work. (2) The team sees that you are human. (3) It gives them permission to lighten up. I have found that when a group can laugh, it becomes a safer place to make mistakes and take risks. Laughter serves as a release from tension and stress. It is even known to strengthen the immune system. Think about work environments you have been in where there was an uptight atmosphere. Compare that with an atmosphere you remember that was more relaxed and fun.

I worked in one Fortune 100 company where people rarely spoke or made eye contact on the elevator. This closed atmosphere permeated through the whole culture, and it didn't surprise me that behind closed doors there was an inordinate focus on office politics, gossip, and other unproductive behaviors.

Even if you are not a naturally "yuck it up" kind of person, you can integrate some lightness and humor into your projects and engage both the introverts and extroverts. The extroverts will respond positively, and the introverts may surprise you. As a project manager you have the power to set the stage.

Here are some other push ideas to build healthy humor into your projects:

1. Celebrate the birthdays of team members each month by bringing breakfast.

2. Bring some "weapons for cubicle warfare," such as foam rubber toys, rubber band guns, air guns, bobble heads, etc. You can buy these at sites such as www.kleargear.com and www.officeplayground.com

3. Go on a team outing such as bowling. Author Dan Pink recommends heading to a children's museum in your area to bring out your right brain.

4. For those of you soured on upbeat motivational sayings, check out www.despair.com. One of their T-shirts says, "More people have read this shirt THAN YOUR BLOG." Their posters say things such as, "Compromise—let's agree to respect each other's views no matter how wrong yours may be." Or how about this poster? A sinking ship is shown with a tag line that says, "It could be the purpose of your life is to serve as a warning to others." My spouse, Bill, drinks his coffee in the morning out of what is called the "pessimist's mug." It has a line across the middle with the accompanying words "The glass is now half empty." Both the extroverts and introverts will smile at that one.

5. Check out the books *301 Ways to Have Fun at Work* and *301 More Ways to Have Fun at Work* for many more ideas.[10]

Practice

As a project manager, you have many opportunities to practice all of the skills discussed in this chapter on a daily basis. Take advantage of the multiple advanced learning opportunities for project managers. Be sure to include a healthy balance of soft and hard skills in

Figure 11. Heading Up Projects Practice

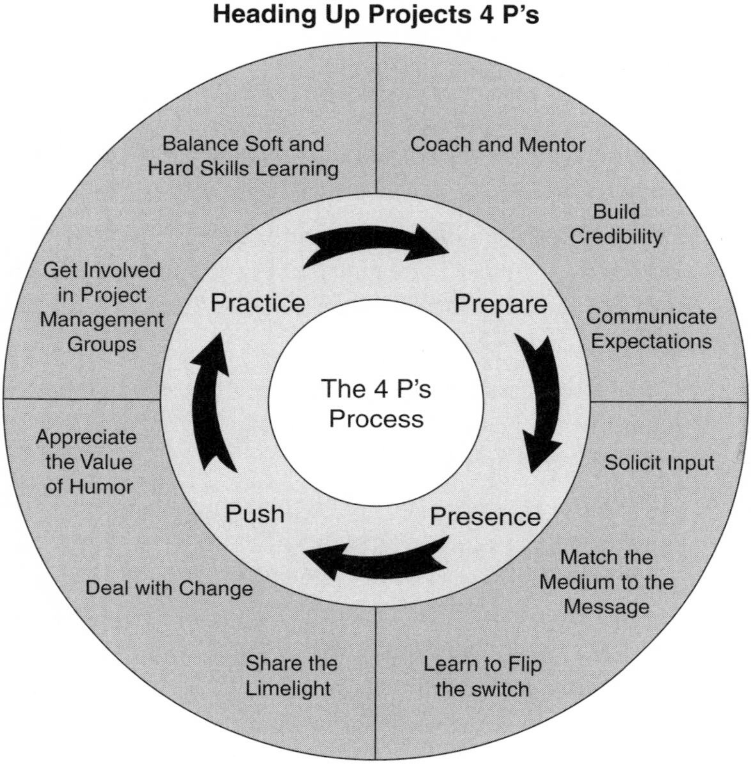

Heading Up Projects 4 P's

your plan, and remember that the people side of the equation is a key to your success.

Also explore becoming a member of a project management association. Such groups can be found across the country, both "live' and online. This will you keep you up on trends, provide continuing education, and will help you develop a vibrant network that you can rely on for feedback. Figure 11 summarizes the steps to enhance your performance as an introverted project manager.

Chapter 7

Managing Up

Jim, the new director of marketing, had barely unpacked the boxes in his office when one by one they marched in. Each of his six direct reports had a list of must-have budget requests. Dianne was the one exception. Instead, she sat and observed the parade of her colleagues. She debated following their lead, but waited and watched as Jim settled into his role. As the weeks went by, Jim didn't request a meeting and, unfortunately, neither did Dianne. It was no surprise that when the budget decisions were made she received less than her peers. Her direct reports were disappointed in the decision but not as much as Dianne. When she finally met with Jim it was too late; the money was already allocated.

Although in some cases this wait-and-see approach is the right strategy, in this situation, Dianne's tentative behavior had detrimental consequences for her and her staff. Not only did they not get needed allocations, but they perceived Dianne as a weak leader. Have you, like Dianne, ever kept silent and lost a critical opportunity? Learning to manage up helps you deal with this challenge. Let's look at what steps Diane could take the next time she is faced with this situation.

Here is what Dianne's task list might have looked like using The 4 P's Process:

Preparation

- Research Jim's background. Do a Google search, and talk with others in the company. Find out about his communication and leadership style in prior jobs.

- Meet with my direct reports to prioritize upcoming goals and budget needs.

- Prepare a sound business case for a budget increase.
- Make a list of questions and talking points for Jim.
- Schedule meeting with Jim.

Presence

- In the meeting, state the purpose, which is to get to know him and be a resource to him. I also will describe my department's needs.
- Listen, ask questions, and build rapport. Match his communication style (e.g., to the point, or more free-flowing).
- Present my boss with a sound business case for budget requests.
- State budget needs and ask when I should check back.
- Smile, be personable, and stick to the time limit.

Push

- Follow up with Jim by the date promised.
- Update my staff on the progress of budget request and other pertinent information.
- Be persistent and timely in my follow-up with Jim.

Practice

- Set up a regular meeting with Jim.
- Continually solicit feedback on my verbal and nonverbal presence with my coaches.
- Practice asking for what I need with other individuals up and across the organization.

Dianne will increase her chances of success with these strategies. She will be more clear and confident in her goals, and, as an introverted leader, close the perception gap with her boss and colleagues.

Let's take a look at how you can stay closely connected to the goals and objectives of your manager. Don't want to play politics?

Think of this as politics with integrity. How can you influence your boss so that you can achieve a stronger partnership and achieve goals for yourself and the people you represent? Peter Drucker said, "You don't have to like or admire your boss, nor do you have to hate him. You do have to manage him, however, so that he becomes your resource for achievement, accomplishment and personal success."[1] Let's look at how you can use the 4 P's to manage up.

Preparation

There is great power in the questions you ask. A salesperson at my former consulting firm often posed a provocative question to prospective clients: "What keeps you up at night?" Asking such questions can give you a clearer understanding of what others are concerned about and what is most important to them so that you can focus your efforts.

With so many restructurings today bosses can change constantly, so having specific questions to ask helps tremendously. Here are some questions you can ask your boss even before you work together and when your direction is unclear.

They fall into three categories: (1) roles and goals; (2) style; and (3) personal development.

1. Roles and Goals Questions

These questions are about your boss's goals, the company's goals, and how she sees you fitting into the big picture. Remember that *your* job is to help her reach *her* goals, and her job is to help her boss. You should first do research to gain as much background as you can about the company, the business, and the competitive landscape so that you can ask intelligent, open-ended questions. Follow-up questions will emerge as you converse.

- How do you see our department supporting the business vision and strategy?
- Do you have a goal document I can see?
- How do you view our current business situation?

- How are we positioned in the marketplace?
- What are our strengths as an organization? Our weaknesses and threats (risks)?
- What are our strengths as a department? Our weaknesses and threats (risks)?
- What are our cost, revenue, and profitability goals? How do you see my role supporting those goals?
- How do the goals of other people who report to you relate to my area? (Note: This question is rarely asked and may uncover potential areas to collaborate with other departments.)
- Here are some of the potential or current challenges I see. How do you suggest we tackle these?
- Here is what would help me in this situation. Can you support me in this area?
- How will you measure success? (Note: Ask for 30-, 60-, and 90-day measures and beyond and offer to draft goals if they don't exist.)

2. Style Questions

Ming was a client. She told me that as a new employee, she had just received a critical feedback review from her manager. When I probed, she revealed that her manager said that Ming was abrupt with other staff people. Over the next week, I suggested Ming be aware of her voice tone and facial expressions in the office and to make eye contact and smile. I also advised her to make special efforts to demonstrate patience with people. At the end of the week, she went into her manager's office and asked if he had noticed an improvement in her behavior. He paused, looked at her with a blank expression on his face, and said that "no news is good news" was his approach to business. To know this approach will be helpful to Ming in managing her boss. She won't expect praise and then be sorely disappointed when she doesn't receive it. I advised her to look for feedback from other sources, including her peers. Last time I checked, she is doing well at work and continuing to manage expectations with her boss.

Temperament and style greatly affect how we communicate with each other. As an introvert, you are probably already a keen observer of style. Pretend you are behind the camera, filming a documentary called *My Boss and Me*. What does his office look like? Does he have family photos, books, and sports memorabilia? Is his desk clean or messy? Is he talking on the phone or e-mailing? Does he prefer voice mail to e-mail? Is he an extroverted, face-to-face person? Is he on the latest smart phone? How is he treating the administrative staff? All of these provide clues about how to successfully connect with him.

How does your boss view the world? Does he talk in facts and details, for example? Myra McElhaney, a corporate trainer, said that in dealing with more analytical bosses you need to tell the boss sales were up by 23 percent instead of saying, "It was a great week," for example.

Does he prepare for meetings at the last minute or days in advance? What about his pace? Is it fast or slow? I had to literally race one of my bosses down the hall to match her high-energy style.

Is she more big picture? Does she sketch out her idea as she talks? One of my introverted clients approached her boss with a model of her thoughts on a four-square table chart. She caught her boss's immediate attention. Follow their cues.

3. Personal Development Questions

If you are not learning you will lose motivation and you will not be contributing fully to your boss and the company. Many bosses are either too busy or unaware of the importance of development conversations. I encourage all my clients to initiate and prepare themselves for that dialogue. What is your next step? Maybe it is to learn new skills, get exposed to a new area of the company, or even step onto a completely different career path. You need to help your boss know how to help you. Make it easy for him to mentor you through thorough preparation.

I ran into Bob Goodyear at a meeting. Bob is an introverted technical product manager at Symantec who prepared for an important meeting by tapping into his courage. One day he went in to see the vice president about making a switch. Bob told me, "I honestly thought that when I graduated from college with a computer science degree that I was going to spend the rest of my life doing nothing more than programming and sitting in a room. . . . I always heard that there were people out there called 'customers' who would actually spend money to buy the products I was working on but I didn't want to go talk to them because they were scary. You know they might tell me that what I was doing was wrong or whatever . . . but when I did one program for the fifth time and it was just in a different programming language, I realized, wait a minute, I don't have a shot of ever getting out of this again if I stay here. I've got to do something different and that's when I took the risk. I got up from my desk, walked in to where the vice president was and said, is there anything else somebody like me can do?" The risk paid off. Bob's career has included stints in sales training and product management, and when I ran into him recently he had a grin on his face because he was on his way to Australia for an assignment.

In the first section of this chapter we looked at questions about roles and goals. Consider these questions about your personal development when approaching your manager.

1. What are the strengths I can use in this role that can help my boss?

2. What projects are good opportunities for me to contribute my skills and background?

3. On which projects can I learn new skills or gain new perspectives?

4. What knowledge, skills, or experience does the boss have that would be valuable for me to learn?

5. Is my boss willing to coach me? How? If he doesn't see that as his role, are there other professionals he would recommend?

Presence

Meeting with your boss regularly is critical. Because her priorities can rapidly change, you need to be ready to recalibrate your own goals and tasks often. You can succeed in managing up by developing presence. This involves three key areas: (1) be yourself; (2) pick low-hanging fruit; and (3) no whining.

1. Be Yourself

Although you have to take responsibility for adjusting to your boss's management and leadership style, you also have to be yourself. When you meet, be sure to solicit feedback from your boss about what is and isn't working. Ask her to be specific about this feedback and prepare specific questions. You may be lucky enough to have a boss who is excellent at giving feedback without prompting. I find that most aren't, but they are trainable. If you initiate the process they may even start asking you for feedback on their work and behaviors.

Respect your manager's time by being focused and clear about your objectives. Think about sending information ahead of time for review. This is especially true if your boss is also introverted. You will build trust that way. Introvert Scott Bynom advised, "Don't be a kiss ass . . . be open and honest. You will build trust that way." In addition I find that some people are intimidated by more senior management. Alex Best, former executive vice president of engineering at Cox Enterprises, advised the following: "Just be yourself. Force yourself to interface with senior management. Have a casual conversation with them and eat lunch with them when it is appropriate. Try to find some common ground and interests. Once you realize that they are really no different than you it becomes much easier to understand where they are coming from and express yourself."

2. Pick Low-Hanging Fruit

Create early results when you are taking on a new job or a new boss. Go for some easier results that you can get in the short term. Can you respond to a customer with a quick fix, or save some costs by sourcing a new supplier? Be sure to document your successes. Managers look for results, so whenever you can take on something that can make even a small impact that is visible, your boss will take notice.

3. No Whining

Come to your boss with solutions, not just problems. Your boss expects you to get the job done without complaining. Seminar participant Luis was a technical professional who felt that he had been unfairly passed over for a promotion. He played the victim, and expected his boss to manage his conflicts with the team. According to Luis, they were frustrating and uncooperative. He complained that they were holding up his deliverables, and he reported this to his boss weekly. The boss offered support, but Luis offered no concrete ideas.

Managers expect you to handle these kinds of issues. Working through conflict is a step-up skill that affects whether your boss sees you as an independent, proactive contributor or not. As of this day, I would put money on the fact that Luis is not seen as a player in his organization, or he is no longer employed there. He did little to close the perception gap. Perhaps he was banished to the basement like Milton Waddams, the character with poor people skills in the movie *Office Space.*[2]

Push

It is not always easy to initiate dialogue upwards, but the alternative is not getting your needs met. Let's look at three push strategies will make this easier over time: (1) speak up; (2) know when not to manage up; and (3) stay on top of change.

1. Speak Up

I ran into a quiet friend recently who I knew was battling cancer. I also was aware that Sasha had a responsible job as a manager of a finance department. When I asked her how she was doing, she said, "Thanks. I am hanging in there and am glad that I pushed myself to have a meeting with my boss. Though my boss is in California and I am on the east coast, and I was advised by my doctors not to push it, I felt the need for a face-to-face conversation about the future. He had given me reassurances about my position and said all was well. But I wanted to see his eyes and hear his voice to determine how he *really* felt about my extended leaves of absence. I shared updates about my plans and how I was handling things back here, and the conversation went better than I ever imagined. I left feeling grateful and proud of myself for opening up the dialogue."

Giving feedback to your boss is also important in a strong partnership. This includes both positive and improvement feedback. None of us can work in a vacuum. We all have blind spots. As managers move up in an organization, they get less feedback about how their actions affect others' performance. Being fearful of your boss's reaction may keep you safe, but it won't help you strengthen the partnership.

So what is a good way to approach the conversation? You can simply say, "May I give you some feedback?" Select an appropriate place, do it soon after the behavior or situation happens, and remember to keep it specific and focused on behaviors. Be sure to suggest an alternative. I like the SAR (AR) approach because it is easy to remember. This means that you first describe the situation (S). Next you describe the action you took (A), and then the result (R) or consequence that occurred because of that action. Then, provide an alternative action (AA), and the alternative result (AR) that could be expected from that action. This is a proposal you are making on how to handle the problem. The goal is to open up a dialogue that is focused on making constructive change, not assigning blame.

Here is an example of feedback you could give to a boss who gives you last minute work to do close to the due date using the SAR approach.

> *Situation—Yesterday I received the weekly report from you to complete by the close of business.*
>
> *Action—I completed it on time. Yet with the tight deadline, I had no time to proof my work.*
>
> *Result—The report went out with potential errors that could slow down our process further down the line.*
>
> *Alternative Action—In the future, I would like to get the weekly report a day earlier.*

Alternative Result—I can produce a quality and error-free document that our department can be proud of.

What are your thoughts?

(Note: The solution or alternative action you agree on may look different after you have a discussion.)

Kelley Robertson, a Canadian sales trainer, shared these helpful comments: "If you have challenges with your manager, it is critical that you address them. Far too many employees bitch, moan, and whine about their boss, but seldom do anything about it." He gave this example:

> In a previous job I began reporting to a different manager who had a completely different style than my previous manager. In addition to expecting face time in the office (I had been used to working from home several days a week), my new manager began micro-managing me. I eventually sat down with him and demonstrated how I could help him reach his goals and achieve better results myself if he let me continue operating the way I had in the past. I made a concession to keep him updated on the projects I was working on. I started with weekly e-mails summarizing my week and highlighting the upcoming week's projects. Eventually, these e-mails became monthly updates. One of the most interesting things I have learned in my career is that many managers have no idea how they are perceived.

2. Know When Not to Manage Up

The caveat is that your boss must be open to receiving feedback. If your manager feels threatened or you are in an organization in turmoil it may not be safe. It could even jeopardize your job. In this case, get coaching from people you respect in the organization about how to handle your manager and remember that you will still learn. In hindsight, many people believe that they actually learn the most from ineffective bosses.

Another situation where managing up may not work is when ethical violations have occurred. I have coached employees who have been asked to do everything from forging company documents to cheating on travel expenses. After they questioned their bosses and the behavior continued, they were forced to report these violations to the appropriate parties. Anne Ball, a nonprofit executive, had a boss who wasn't honest with himself or others. He was cynical, puerile, capricious, self-absorbed, and unethical. No amount of 'managing upward' can overcome that kind of individual.

If you are in one of these situations where trust has been broken, you will likely become frustrated and lose motivation. Then it is time to consider what other career options you may have.

3. Stay on Top of Change

I have said that knowing your boss's top three priorities helps you to manage your own work and decide what to focus on so that you are supporting her in the best way possible. Working from her goal sheet will put you on the same page.

Communicating with your boss also lets you keep the dialogue open about changes in the company. It allows you to bring her ideas and trends you have heard about. I taught an introverted Six Sigma Black Belt professional named Serg in one of my classes. He shared that though he was new in his company role, he was achieving credibility with his boss. Serg said that because he was doing work on global cross-functional project teams, he was able to collect valuable customer data and innovations that he then fed back to his department. It kept him on the cusp of change. Serg quickly became a person that people wanted on their teams, and his boss appreciated how Serg helped the entire department achieve visibility and presence.

Practice

Managing your boss is a combination of science and art. (See Figure 12.) There are some guidelines, but there is wide latitude in execution. By meeting regularly, asking questions, and providing feedback, you will ensure that your mutual goals are met. As your managers change you should continue to drive communication

Figure 12. Managing Up Practice

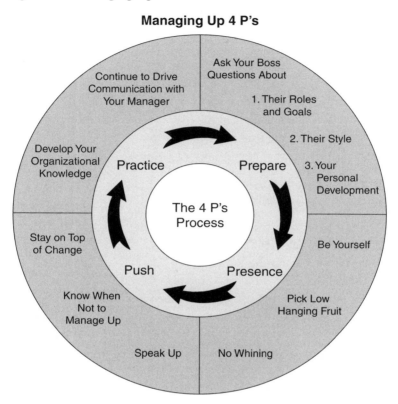

Managing Up 4 P's

whenever and however possible. It is the only way you will know if you are on target and what steps you can take to correct yourself when you are off course.

In addition, keep up your organizational knowledge so that your goals are consistent with the direction of your company. You will continue to become a valued partner to your boss as you face the future.

Chapter 8

The Meeting Game

Carlos, an account executive, dialed in for the weekly conference call. As the initial chit chat transpired, he convinced himself that this time it would be different. With many extroverted callers in his nationwide group, he often found it difficult to get the boss to listen to his ideas. This time he was determined to get heard. The high-energy group started in and raced through the agenda. When asked to give his report Carlos did fine, but after the back-and-forth dialogue began on the new marketing plan, he found himself overanalyzing his potential answers. By the time he was ready to speak up, the group had moved on to the closing business, and Carlos had missed his chance to share his expertise on the Western region. More importantly, he also lost the chance to be seen as a player by his boss and co-workers. Carlos's goal of participation was on target. So was his thoughtful analysis. Where he failed was in execution, in stepping out there and having the confidence to let his ideas be heard.

Like Carlos, do you ever feel invisible in meetings? If you are introverted, clamming up and feeling intimidated is common, especially around lots of extroverted people. When your ideas and input do not get recognized, you can lose out by (1) not being credited for your contributions, (2) having your ideas preempted or hijacked by others, or (3) being perceived as not adding much value to the group.

Your career can be charged up or deflated by how you act and perform in meetings. In one study conducted by Hofstra University,[1] four out of five managers evaluated each other based on how they participated in meetings. Eighty-seven percent of the people studied assess a person's strength of leadership based on how they run a meeting. There are personal benefits to you as well. Who wants to waste their time in a meeting with no focus or results? Organizations benefit when meetings are run well. It is estimated that managers spend more than one-quarter of their time in meetings, and that organizations spend more than 60 billion dollars a year in unproductive meetings! What a waste of dollars and people power.

So let's take a look at what you can do as an introverted leader to make your meetings work. Carlos, in our earlier example, could have used the 4 P's Process to establish his seat at the table. He might have done a few things differently. He could have avoided being bowled over by interjecting comments at opportune points and by writing down some points as they were being said so that he could be concise, cogent, and clear in his responses. Let's look at how you can master meetings using the 4 P's Process.

Prepare

Successful introverted leaders strategize for people interactions. It helps to look at meetings as a game, not in the "back-door office politics" way, but like a game of tennis. When you play a competitive sport, you first have to learn the game. You may start by watching a few matches, taking lessons, and getting a grasp of the rules, including how to keep score. As you gain mastery, you also learn how to size up your opponents and develop a strategy. You may think, "If they are weak in their backhand, I will hit my shots there" or "I need to run into the net if I notice them hanging out in the back court." This is what makes you a strong player (in addition to natural ability). It is similar with planning for meetings. You need to prepare before the meeting: (1) know the purpose, (2) have an agenda, and even (3) plan where to sit and stand.

Before the Meeting "Game"
1. Know the Purpose

What is the desired outcome for the meeting? Is it to tell the group about a decision or to sell one? Is it to make the decision? Is the purpose to solve a problem, create ideas, vent feelings, or recognize achievements? Unless there is a clear target for what you want to accomplish, then it will be guaranteed to be an inefficient and ineffective meeting.

What is the reason *you* have been asked to attend? Were you copied on the invite list out of habit? If your boss delegated you to be there in her absence, are you empowered to make decisions? If not, then your presence can actually slow down the meeting process because decisions will be held up until your boss weighs in.

2. Have an Agenda

Going to a meeting without an agenda is like going sailing on a ship without sonar, there is no frame of reference and no way to measure progress. You will sail in circles because you may be thinking it is not your role to push for this. But it is, if you value your time and career. You can "manage up" by asking the team leader to provide an agenda so that you can be better prepared to fully contribute to the meeting. You can also offer to prepare the agenda and run it by your manager or team leader. This is a great way of stepping up, and will help you be more confident about the remarks you want to make during the meeting.

An introvert who knew his style, shared: "A former boss of mine, an extrovert, and I developed a rather nice system. . . . . Before a critical meeting, he would come by my office and drop off a written proposal. He would then leave and say, 'I need you to look at this. I will be back in five or ten minutes.' This one action helped us both tremendously. He gave me time to study the issue internally, and by coming back he could toss his thoughts in the air and be in his zone as well."

3. Get Your Voice in the Room

When you know (1) what you are expected to contribute, (2) the desired outcome of the meeting, and (3) the other participants who will be there, you can plan your strategy and comments. You should also plan on getting your first comment heard no more than 5 minutes into the meeting. Get your "voice in the room," because the longer you wait, the bigger a deal it becomes. You will feel like you have to say something profound or perfect. Making a comment, question, or even paraphrasing what has been said is easier to do in the beginning, and you will be perceived as a contributor. Practice your remarks in the mirror ahead of time if this thought paralyzes you. With practice and focus, you will make it happen.

4. Plan Where to Sit and Stand

In live meetings be smart about where you sit. Kimberly Douglas, CEO of Firefly Facilitation, recommends that you sit a few seats away from the leader and resist your tendency to hide in the back of the room.

What about on conference calls? Don't sit, *stand*. Yes, even though people can't see you, they will hear more energy in your voice. Standing up is proven to make your voice more robust as your diaphragm opens and you breathe in more oxygen. Also get on the call a little early. Plan on engaging in some initial chit-chat with the leader and other members. This rapport building will help substantially when you get to the real give and take of the meeting. Your presence will already be established. It becomes even more important to use your voice and words to establish strong communication on conference calls because you don't have visual cues.

Presence—Play the Meeting Game

This section introduces ways of establishing presence in playing the meeting game: (1) set ground rules; (2) use creative techniques to involve members; and (3) separate brainstorming from decision making.

1. Set Ground Rules

Let's return to the tennis analogy. When you play a game like tennis, what counts is how you perform on the court. The wind may be strong, or your ankle can hurt, but you need to keep hitting winners. Similarly, in the meeting game, conditions can change, but ultimately meetings thrive or die based on the way they are run. If you want to make sure that your meetings are more productive, I suggest you try out some ground rules at your next meeting.

Ground rules (see Figure 13) are guidelines the team agrees to follow. They help to put some controls on the meeting process.

Here are a few considerations with ground rules. (1) Consider your ethnic and organizational culture. In Asian countries, for instance, it would not work to have a rule about "speaking in headlines." The norm is to encourage consensus and group discussion. (2) Discuss the rules and get buy-in from the group. Make sure the wording fits and that the meaning is clear to everyone.

As a meeting leader you can get commitment by asking people to do a thumbs-up or thumbs-down if they agree or disagree with the proposed rules. A few minutes can be taken at the end of the session for people to weigh in and make suggestions for the next time. Request that everyone write down one thing they thought went well about the meeting and one thing to improve. This can include comments about the meeting room temperature or the scope of the project. You can read the comments out loud and ask for clarification if needed. Suggestions for fixes can be made then, or you can make adjustments between meetings to respond to the feedback.

Figure 13. Sample Ground Rules

Sample Ground Rules

- Be on time—start and stop time of the meeting, back from breaks and agenda items
- Participate—with your mouth and in your head
- Show respect—no side conversations and one person at a time
- Cell phones and Blackberries on silent—that includes vibrations
- No laptops—takes away focus from the meeting
- Speak in headlines—focus on main points
- Confidentiality—what is said stays in the room
- Silence—gives us time to shuffle our thoughts

Be willing to enforce the rules. One group I know had a "be on time" ground rule. They decided to lock the door once the meeting started. Everyone agreed and the door was locked at future meetings, causing some anticipated surprise from several team members. They were on time in subsequent meetings!

2. Use Creative Techniques to Involve Members

Good tennis coaches use a variety of different drills to improve technique. Team leaders do the same thing when they initiate "right-brain" strategies that play to the preferences of introverts in addition to other practice. We are all familiar with brainstorming. A technique called "brain writing" is a variation on this technique that can work well with introverts. Put a problem at the top of a sheet and ask for solutions. Pass it around the table. The first person puts their idea on the sheet, and the next person builds on it and/or writes a new idea. The ideas that emerge are usually more robust than if spoken on the fly. The brain has time to marinate and is stimulated by other ideas. Check out www.aboutyouinc.com for more ideas on customizing brainstorming techniques for the preferences of both introverts and extroverts.

3. Separate Brainstorming from Decision Making

Since introverts often want time to process information before they weigh in, schedule two separate meetings to handle these two functions. Or if time is of the essence, or it is an all-day meeting, take an extended break and give people time to get away from the table. This is a good idea to do in general. The right side of our brain, the creative and emotional side, works separately from the left side, which is responsible for more logical processing and logical thinking. Breaks allow us to leverage the capabilities of our whole brain.

Martin Schmidler has figured out a way to manage this with his team members. When they want a decision from him he buys some time by telling them that he will respond the next day. People are usually fine with that response. "It is all how I frame it up," he says.

Push

Take your meetings to the next level with three push considerations: (1) technology as friend and foe; (2) get involved; and (3) take the floor.

1. Technology as Friend and Foe

During drills, my tennis coach brought orange cones to encourage us to place the ball all around the court. On game day, however, the props were gone. We were to focus on being in the game itself. Technology, like those orange cones, can be a huge distraction in meetings. Extroverts and introverts can lose focus this way. Many introverts are comfortable communicating through e-mail, instant messaging, text messages, and social networking sites. They may also let these tools disrupt concentration at meetings.

However, there has been resistance. In some organizations, people are prohibited from bringing their laptops into the meeting room. An article in the *L.A. Times*[2] referred to this method as "going topless." According to the article, John Vars, co-founder of Dogster Inc., decided that bringing computers into meetings was "not in keeping with their philosophy of creating a collaborative culture. Even if people are just taking notes, they are not giving the natural human signals that they are listening to the person who is speaking. It builds up resentment. . . . Now people are communicating better and the flow is faster." One client told me that his team has a "no mute button" rule on conference calls, and this discourages participants from multitasking, encouraging them to be more fully present.

Using technology in a meeting can even cost lost sales. I was told that on one conference call, several folks came up with a great idea while the customer was talking. They decided to put this customer on hold to discuss "their brilliant proposal," not knowing that while they did so, that customer outlined the exact same idea. When they returned to the call and presented their innovative concept, they were embarrassed to be caught in the act of truly not listening. There was some backpedaling to do.

On the other hand, technology can be an asset at meetings. Mary Orr, a marketing manager at a Fortune 50 company, told me about her experience using instant messaging. She said that, often, meeting participants will send each other a quick instant or text message to make sure they are on the same page before they pitch an idea to a client or senior executive. This is a kind of "techie check-in." She and others find this a great way of touching base and streamlining communication.

The growth of virtual technology, such as Web meetings, webinars, and virtual classrooms, allows interaction and visual prompts. These services are highly interactive as they allow for instant feedback to meeting leaders. Introverts may feel more comfortable using this technology because they can respond in written form and at a pace that is more comfortable to them. On the other hand, the relative safety of not having to be in contact with people may encourage disengagement and invisibility. Push yourself by maintaining a live presence. Contribute questions and comments at regular intervals and respond to the online surveys that are often included in these virtual meetings.

2. Get Involved

The introvert's proclivity for listening and observing can really help here. First, you can observe yourself. Are you being present or are you checking out? Are certain folks dominating the meeting? Push yourself to speak up and also engage others. After all, the reason for having a meeting is to get the best thinking of everyone. If you are the meeting leader, you can take charge here. Figure 14 lists some practical push strategies that you can implement or recommend to the meeting leader as a meeting participant.

3. Take the Floor

As for Carlos in the earlier example, pushing also means getting heard despite resistance from talkers. Be prepared with your facts and be ready to jump in if you need to. Here are other push tips shared by successful introverted leaders when others are saying more than their share.

Figure 14. Techniques for Involvement

Techniques for Involvement

- Volunteer to take a role as scribe, timekeeper, etc.

- If someone has not spoken in a while, say their name and ask them what they think.

- Put a question out to the group and structure the responses. Tell people that each person will get 2 minutes to give their opinion on the topic, and keep to the time.

- On conference calls and Web meetings, go from east to west or in alphabetical order. Use the whiteboard function to have them identify their location. Ask people to weigh in on a topic.

- Write it down. Before your discussions, in either live or remote meetings, ask people to take 2-3 minutes to jot down their thoughts. You can use meeting technology to share responses. The extroverts may be impatient but, they will live! You will find the input to be much richer. In the last meeting I ran, I played some soft music for our thinking break, and it worked beautifully.

- Break the team into smaller groups (no more than four to six people) to discuss problems and report back with a response. You will feel the energy in the room palpably rise and hear the introverts' voices in there with everyone else's. I have done this hundreds of times, and it is a foolproof method for involvement.

Tips for Handling Talkers at Meetings

- Don't smile or nod your head in agreement. That only encourages the long-winded participant. Maintain a flat expression.

- Don't get into a shouting match out of frustration. Offer to discuss the topic offline or table the discussion until things cool down.

- Hold up your hand with the stop signal, especially if a talker is going on and on. Then say, "I would like to say something."

- If cut off, take a cue from the pundits on the news shows' split screens. In a strong voice say, "I am speaking and would like to finish my thought."

- Prepare and make your comments with confidence. "Look them in the eye," Trina Thompson, director of help desk operations at Advance America, told me. "They can smell it when you are not prepared."

- If you miss your opportunity in the meeting, don't hesitate to talk to the person afterward. Trina learned that "a sidebar is better than nothing." They then know you have something to contribute, and they are more likely to bring you out the next time and consult with you outside the meeting because they know what you can contribute.

Practice—Mastering Meetings

Picture this: You are attending meetings where your input is valued. Everyone wants you on their team. Action items are executed that move projects forward. Your career benefits from gaining visibility with others across and outside your organization. You are perceived as a superhero because you have freed up time for people to actually accomplish their work because they aren't stuck in meetings all day. Your company is reaping millions of dollars in cost savings from the efficiency of its meetings.

Does this sound like a pipe dream? It is possible, and even likely to happen, if you practice your skills in the meeting game (see Figure 15).

You can become *a meeting subject matter expert*. Most technical folks are familiar with the subject matter expert concept. Because the majority of organizations seem to lack the fundamentals of basic meeting management, why not bring in different ways of approaching meetings? You can be the one to create agendas, establish ground rules, and champion some other involvement techniques that we have discussed. These can be small changes that make a huge difference in moving your meetings forward.

Take the example of Janine, a recent client. She is an introverted IT director at a large wireless phone provider who has had a track record of promotions. Janine had just joined a group of peers who ran pretty dysfunctional meetings. At times, even shouting matches occurred. She was not one to yell back though she could certainly hold her own. Janine was frustrated because she knew meetings didn't have to be an energy drainer. She felt compelled to take action.

As a first step, Janine met with the team lead privately and suggested he post some ground rules at the next meeting. He agreed and got buy-in from the group. Janine told me that the ground rule "One person speaks at a time" figured prominently on the list. People started listening to each other. Slowly meetings started getting back on track. Though they still disagreed on many issues, the ground rules helped them work through the disagreements.

Figure 15. The Meeting Game Practice

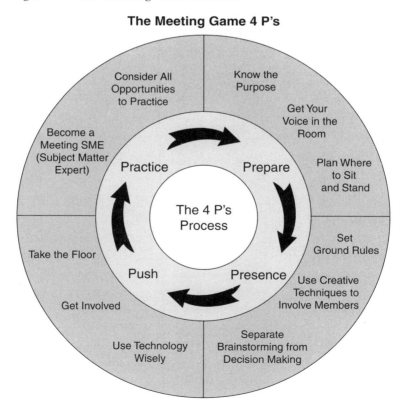

As a second step toward progress, Janine offered to coordinate a series of interactive training programs that would get people of all levels in the department together. She thought the topics of time and project management would help them build skills. She felt that the real win, however, would be the chance to have discussions in a non-threatening atmosphere.

I was privileged to facilitate the first session when this formerly hostile group actually built a tower together. We debriefed the lively group dynamics. The teams were talking and laughing, and I could only think that would not have occurred if one effective introverted leader had not pushed herself out of her natural style.

If you work in any kind of job, opportunities to practice your meeting skills exist all around you. Consider other opportunities in volunteer or sports organizations, where you can apply meeting skills. You can even practice at family gatherings. Roberto Vargas book *Family Activism* describes how meeting tools can strengthen families. Once you've achieved meeting mastery you will not go back.

Chapter 9

Building Relationships

It was time for the annual customer retreat at a nice resort in Hawaii. John, a new IT account executive, quickly retrieved his suitcase from the baggage carousel and headed to the taxi line. Then he noticed that most of his group was waiting for their golf clubs to arrive. Because he had played only a few times, John figured that his golf handicap was too high to play with this group of mostly experienced golfers. His plan was to go for a run and a nap while the others were hitting the back nine that afternoon.

He followed his agenda, and was feeling pretty relaxed when he walked into the next morning's new product rollout meeting. However, John quickly realized that he was missing out on some of the jokes from the previous day's outing. It was also apparent that some customer concerns about the product features had come up in golf course discussions and were being referenced in a number of the comments. He felt like he was playing catch-up, at the start. Unfortunately, John had not realize that the unwritten rules of his company included some involvement in "offline" activities such as golf. He would have some catching up to do.

Have you ever found that things have been decided at the "meeting before the meeting?" Information is shared, connections are strengthened, and decisions get made in these important pre-meetings. In today's corporate world, the golf course, the company gym, or the local coffee shop serves as the backdrop for much of this business. Sponsored community events such as road races or bike rides, and volunteer projects such as Habitat for Humanity, are also potential settings for these unofficial discussions. Conferences and trade shows are other venues where deals get made out of the official limelight.

As an introvert, you may go into "shut down" mode every time one of these mingling opportunities comes up. You also probably cringe when people say things like, "If you don't schmooze, you lose." Networking is the building of relationships for mutual exchange. It is necessary, but it is *not* natural for most introverts.

Jay Conger and N. Anand said in an excellent article called "Capabilities of the Consummate Networker," "Without fail, the managers who are most effective at networking that we researched told us they worked hard at developing their networking skills. It required a serious investment of time and focus on their part. . . . It is not a birthright of the chosen few."[1] Introverts can still be strong relationship builders by working at it. The two are not mutually exclusive. Let's look at how you can use the 4 P's Process to build relationships.

Prepare

Preparing to build relationships means you should: (1) know your purpose; (2) plan what you have to offer; (3) plan what you need; (4) use social networking to set the stage; and (5) defeat negative self-talk.

1. Know Your Purpose

If you don't know where you are going, any road will take you there. John, in our example, should have been clear about his desired outcomes for the event. Perhaps he wanted to learn about his customer Mario's needs. Or maybe he needed to know what Catherine's issue was with his service area's turnaround time.

Who should you target for networking? Consider the influencers in your meeting. Plan to have a conversation, sit with them at dinner, and seek out kingpins at the cocktail reception.[2] These are the people who determine expectations for performance and influence others.

Social settings also can be windows into the personal style of others. Golfers, for instance, have told me that they learn more about a person's values in a relaxed setting such as the golf course than at work. I have heard of business deals blown by a player throwing down his club at a missed shot or otherwise violating etiquette. A colleague, Tom, told me about a client who became inebriated each time the bar rolled out at company receptions. Tom learned to work around this client in order to get new business. As an introvert and keen observer of behavior, he learned who not to target in this situation.

If John, in the earlier example, had written down his goals for the retreat, his experience might have differed. His intention and focus would be on listening and learning more about specific customer needs. He may have even chosen to play golf or meet the group afterward, given that most of the group was planning on being there. He would have gleaned targeted information that could help him and his company solve problems of concern to the client.

Introverts have told me that writing down their agenda and questions beforehand was critical in preparing for spontaneous encounters at the bar, in the boardroom, or in the elevator. Having prepared questions in his head, John could have moved strictly social conversations into ones that got needed answers to important questions.

2. Plan What You Have to Offer

Connecting is a process of mutual exchange, so you need to first know what you have to offer other people in interactions. Consider both work and non–work-related resources, information, experience, expertise, and ideas. Have you discovered a cool new technology tool such as Skype that you can share with people? Have you taken a day trip to a new children's museum that the kids loved? Have you discovered yoga and seen some benefits that you would like to share? What have you been learning about lately that fascinates you? Read a book or seen a film that captivated you? Even if people don't take advantage of your suggestions now they know who to tap later on when that information or resource is needed. So put it out there. You will probably be animated and enthusiastic when you speak about your interests. You will also come across as more of a real person, a person of depth. Offering your best self will make you someone with whom others want to continue the conversation, not make the quickest exit.

3. Plan What You Need

After you consider what you have to offer, reflect upon your own needs. What resources, information, or expertise do you require now in your life? Consider a flexible series of needs in your head and be prepared to bring out relevant items as the conversation evolves. Just as John could have prepared with specific questions for his customer at the golf retreat, you should prepare questions that target your goals.

What do you want to learn? An introverted work colleague told me about a wall he was coming up against at work. He had diagnosed the cause of this to be his own avoidance of conflict, and he asked me to recommend classes and books to increase his range of assertive communication. I was glad to know how specifically I could help him.

What about life outside of work? Let's say you are in a dual-career partnership, and both of you have heavy work schedules. You learn that your client is in the same situation. You might ask for resources that they have found to save time in preparing meals.

Even if you don't find the exact right answer to your challenge, by disclosing something as a need, you connect on another level. You are more than customer and client; you become two people trying to muddle through the ups and downs of a jam-packed life. Of course, you have to gauge if someone is open to discussing non-work matters, but I have found most people welcome the chance for this back-and-forth problem solving about issues that affect them at the core.

4. Use Social Networking and E-mail to Set the Stage

The great news about technology is that it can turn calls from cold to warm. T. Daniel Martin, a community manager, finds social networking sites to be a great preparation tool for introverts before meeting in person. "I have two people on my sales team who are incredible introverts," he said. "One of them is always in our top sales tier. They use online social networking as a means of creating a 'warm' relationship with the client before they make any type of personal contact. They send an initial invite to an event, or a copy of a report, and then follow up with an e-mail. It is a nonthreatening excuse for an introduction, to say something such as: 'Have you received an invitation yet to . . .' or 'Mr. Smith, I wanted to make sure you got a copy of . . . .' The item or invite has to be something of value, but that normally breaks the introvert's fear and/or reluctance over making contact." Gerry Mann, an introverted director, shared his advice. "Be prepared to ask questions ('What is the most interesting part of your job?') as well as talk about yourself ('I like chocolate-covered cherries') and your interests ('I collect maps in foreign languages'). Find some common ground and work from there, or find a *difference* ('I've never been scuba diving, what was the hardest part to learn?') and learn something new. As this book is being written, Facebook, LinkedIn, and many other social networking sites are increasingly in use. Make these a part of your networking strategy, but don't have them replace face-to-face contact.

5. Replace Negative Self-Talk

Often it is the self-defeating committee in our heads that keeps us on the sidelines (see Figure 16). Each of us has to find ways to overcome the fears that can incapacitate us in building relationships. First we need to become aware of what those committee members are saying, and then we need to examine the validity of these statements. Then it becomes a process of replacing those self-defeating thoughts with positive ones.

Let's consider the negative internal statements and replacement statements for John in our earlier example.

The trick is to catch yourself when you are being hijacked by the negative members of the committee in your head. Ask yourself, "What am I telling myself about this?" and then counter that negative talk with a positive counter response.

If you do this kind of mindshift in the prepare stage, the bulk of the work is done. In summary, spend some time getting to know your purpose, plan what you have to offer and your needs, use technology such as social networking ahead of time, and replace negative self-talk with positive statements. Also remember to take time to recharge your batteries before people-oriented encounters. Unlike

Figure 16. Internal Committee Statements

Replacing Negative Statements

Negative Internal Statement	Replacement Statements
I don't have any ability at the game.	I can take lessons. or There are handicaps for golfers like me. or I don't know about my ability until I try.
I am uncomfortable making small talk.	I can get more comfortable by preparing questions ahead of time. or I can do some research beforehand to learn about my golfing partners (i.e., Do they have kids? If so, what are their ages? Do they have pets? Where do they live? How long they have been playing the game?)
I feel guilty about not playing yet I hate golf. Why must I conform to the group pressure to play?	I don't have to. I can go for a run and meet the group for drinks afterwards and catch up on the latest buzz. I can make a point to talk to Mario and Catherine there.

your extroverted colleague, whose battery is charged up by interactions, *your* battery needs time to regenerate and recharge.

Presence

So are you psyched up to network? Or like Bob Goodyear, the Symantec technical products manager, are you ready to "endure it"? He said, "It [talking with people] is just part of the job." Sharon Schierling, a coach, said, "For an introvert networking in large crowds is right up there with poking their eyes with hot needles, but most introverts do very well one- on-one."

This section includes some ideas about how to make an impression with customers and clients. You develop presence by being able to do four key things: (1) listen; (2) engage in substance talk rather than small talk; (3) learn and teach names; and (4) answer the question, "So what do you do?"

1. Listen

Dale Carnegie said, "You can make more friends in two months by becoming interested in other people than in two years by trying to get other people interested in you." Because introverts focus on depth versus breadth and listen well, they can build on this listening strength and segue into a conversation that reveals true interest in the other person. The questions you prepare help you to listen.

My spouse Bill, the introvert, is a professor. I often run into his former students around town. They usually comment first on his quirky sense of humor. Next, they tell me stories about the genuine interest he showed in them. One told me how Bill helped him think through a career choice. Another told me how Bill helped him sort through a personal dilemma with focused attention. Hard to read and even gruff sometimes on the outside, his insides are gentle and kind. He is a sometimes-misunderstood introvert, but what people pick up is his strong ability to listen and connect. It is a huge asset, and one that obviously has made a lasting impression on these graduates.

2. Substance Talk vs. Small Talk

Substance talk, as opposed to small talk, is what leads to connections. Conversations may start out small (e.g., talking about the weather), but you can then segue into a topic of mutual interest. For instance, I found myself discussing some tornadoes that had struck near my area. The man I was speaking with proceeded to give me a detailed description of these events, and we both lamented the damage to the downtown area. I then transitioned to discussing the CNN center, so I was able to share with him the effects of the winds on one of my clients, Turner Broadcasting. That led to a focused discussion of his experience with that company, and we discovered that we had some common contacts. At this point we were in substance talk. Breaking the ice is important. Tom Bormand, a technical recruiter, said, "I have always relied on finding common ground to start the conversations. . . . Just anything to get the other person to talk more about them, as that is what you are after in networking. Maybe it's the weather, sports, movies, or where they're from. It's funny that most people are introverts themselves at these events, so I look to be the one who takes the burden to break the ice."

3. Learn and Teach Names

Did you know that 97 percent of people say they cannot remember names? Yet it makes such a difference when someone calls us by name. Learning names is not as easy as it once was. Pronunciation is a lot more complicated, so be sure to ask people how to pronounce their name. Ask them what they like to be called. Do they have a nickname?

Remembering names is probably not as hard for John from our example at the customer retreat as it might be in large venues where there are a great deal of new people. Name tags help. Successful salespeople are terrific at names. Here are some tips that I have learned from watching them.

- Use a name repeatedly. Even if you don't say it out loud, say it in your head. You can actually tell your brain that a name is important to store by repeating it.

- Associate the person's name with someone else by that name, and superimpose that image on the person's face when you are speaking with them. Jim Ziegler, a professional speaker, says he can remember 100+ names at a time using this method.

- Connect the name with a tangible object. Jane E. Brody, *New York Times* health columnist, writes, "I associate a new name with a tangible object: Cucumber for Kirby . . . ravioli for Ralph and 'sherry' for Sherry.[2] A man named Ragu was in a seminar I taught recently. I did not forget his name all week. Can you guess why? The spaghetti sauce association was so easy!"

Teaching your name provides an opportunity to be remembered. Use the Forest Gump rule. (Remember, he said, "Forest, Forest Gump.") Lynn Waymon and Anne Baber, in *Making Contacts Count*,[3] referenced Sherry Hunter, who tells people, "Sherry Hunter. Sherry like the drink. You can remember Hunter because I hunt down computer problems and fix them."

Other useful mnemonic devices include remembering what a name rhymes with or what it sounds like. I sometimes focus on the pronunciation and spelling of my name because that is what is hard to remember. I will say, "It's Kahnweiler with a K." Then I say, "K A H N, pronounced Kahn, W E I, pronounced Why (because I am always asking why)," and then I will spell out, "L-E-R." A friend told me I should say my name rhymes with "Rottweiler." You should stay away from negative connotations, so I am not sure what her underlying message to me was!

4. So, What Do You Do?

You will inevitably be asked to respond to the question, "What do you do?" Especially from people who don't know you. Forget crafting a canned elevator speech. Keep it real. People want to hear simple language that they can understand.

Use a three-part formula: (1) "I am" (your position or profession); (2) "who does" (what you do); and (3) "for example." This last part is the most important. Allow your listener to get a visceral feel for what you do by providing an accomplishment or story. John, the man from our example, could have maintained presence at his company retreat by having a great answer to this question. Here is how the dialogue might sound:

Tonya (a sales rep from the client company): "So John, what do you do?"

John: I am an account executive, Tonya. My job is to understand the needs of your company and translate those changing requirements from you to our support teams. For example, your facility in Portland had an increase in production, and I worked with the plant manager to provide some just-in-time training for the team. As a result they didn't skip a beat and exceeded their production goals. Have you had any experience working with our software?

John's answer includes some additional items to keep in mind. He uses Tonya's name as he responds. This is particularly beneficial because you're most often asked this question by people you have just met. Also, he plans his answer to lead into a question related to his purpose.

Push

Stepping out of your comfort zone can take a number of forms when it is part of your job to win over new prospects and strengthen ties with existing customers.

For John, push might have meant offering to move out of his typical role. Volunteering to help by organizing the golf round robin or by planning the retreat program would have cast him in a more visible light and forced him to interact with different people. Relationships will build naturally that way. Because networking is more about who knows you than who you know, your visibility will increase. Here is a list of six practical push tips for introverts to help you build and manage relationships with clients and customers, both in your organization and in the larger world.

Push Tips for Building Relationships

1. It is worth repeating here what introverted leaders have consistently told me. They act the part. Whether the imagined role is James Bond or the host or hostess of a party, or even imagining wearing a costume, pretending lessens the nervousness. When you start acting, the brain takes over and believes that you really are confident! So act "as if."

2. Strike up conversations with people in line at the grocery store, doing errands, etc. You never know where these conversa-

tions can lead, especially if you keep in mind what you have to offer and your needs, to direct these interactions toward substantive communication.

3. Schedule visits or call customers when you are in a location for another purpose. They will appreciate the attention and you will learn more about their needs and save money.

4. At a dinner or luncheon, use the opportunity to start what Sam Horn calls a "table top" conversation.[4] Tell the group that you will start and then each person can give a 2-minute overview of what they are involved in right now, or what they think of the program topic, etc. You will make new networking connections and be perceived as proactive.

5. Stay close to comfortable socializers. An introvert in medical sales told me that in the real world she latches onto a social butterfly and connects through their connections.

6. Volunteer for a professional, business, or community organization. Don't just be a "card carrying member," because you can meet a lot of people with similar interests in your niche and showcase your strengths and talents.

Practice

As you develop presence and push to expand your networking skills (see Figure 17), add practice in these areas: (1) safe environments first and (2) keep your Web presence current.

1. Safe Environments First

Laura Sherman, a mortgage director, has an interesting approach to training introverts to be salespeople:

> I recruit and train people into a business that requires constantly building up a warm market. It is hard for introverts, so I created an exercise. I get people to practice just starting conversations about anything, like an article of clothing, and ask questions like, "I really like your shirt. Where did you get it?" Then have them

be genuinely interested in the answer, really listen, and ask a question based on the answer (i.e., Answer: "Ross" "Oh really, I like to shop there too. Did you catch the sale last week?").

Introverted people do need more work and they need to work on the first step for many hours, but it really does help. They usually realize it isn't so scary when you put your attention on talking to the other person and helping them!

Practicing these skills in a safe and comfortable atmosphere leads to results. You may not be in sales, but you too can start small and gain confidence in this process.

Figure 17. Building Relationships Practice

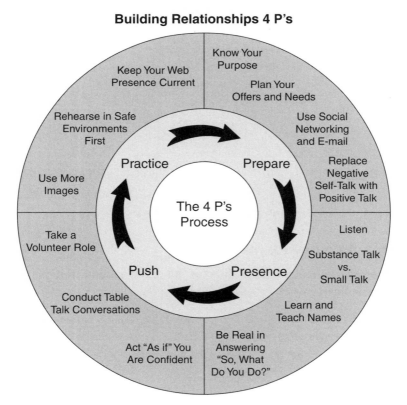

2. Keep Your Web Presence Current

Manage your online profiles and connections. Introverts cite this as a preferred way to propel their connections forward because it doesn't require intense face-to-face contact, which is a draining proposition. Many introverted leaders recommend using blogging as a way for people to become familiar with your name and your expertise. Writing articles and blogs are ways to position yourself in your industry and field. You will have more of a Web presence, and a wider variety of people both in and outside your field will learn your name. Jason Slater, an IT manager, wrote me a note on LinkedIn (appropriately!). He said, "I have found that creating a blog offered a useful outlet and way of networking and expressing my thoughts and interests as I seem to be a far better communicator 'in text' rather than 'in person.'

Chapter 10

Wins from Using the 4 P's Process

Wins for You

Preparation

Raj stared down at the phone receiver. He knew he had to pick it up. Now that his consulting firm had imposed a sales quota for each financial consultant, he had to make the next call. He decided to call Michelle, a former client, to touch base and uncover her current business needs. As he pressed the numbers on his handset, he reviewed the questions he had prepared and his desired outcome for the conversation: an appointment. Raj visualized a successful call by closing his eyes for 2 minutes and pictured a calm, focused exchange between them. As the phone rang, he took a deep breath and stood up (a method he had learned in sales training to improve his voice quality). Michelle picked up. After 10 minutes of give and take, he summarized the challenges she had described, and they set a time to meet the following week. Raj felt energized and optimistic about future business opportunities with Michelle and her company, and that afternoon he even found himself whistling in his cube.

Like Raj, have you found that even a small amount of preparation can boost your confidence and reduce your anxiety? Of course, we all can procrastinate tasks that don't come naturally to us, but Raj pushed himself to engage. By reflecting on your purpose, your conversations can become much more productive. Raj also attended a class in sales training, which helped him with his presence. Even a small amount of preparation for the call allowed him to manage his stress and be present with Michelle. He didn't worry about what he was going to say next, but could listen to her and engage in a fruitful conversation that yielded his desired result: an appointment. Preparation was key. Taking notes also made it possible to refer back to them later when he needed them. Sid Milstein, the introverted senior executive, said that by preparing questions you are learning more than those who wing it, and you are creating a positive impression.

Let's take a closer look at some additional payoffs of having presence.

Presence

Being present helps you manage stress and close the perception gap. If Mady, the overworked employee in chapter 1, had cleared her mind for a few minutes, or even taken a mental health day, she might have become more aware of the extent of her exhaustion. This also could have helped her to take a clearer, rational look at her situation and take subsequent action.

One of the benefits of doing yoga and other similar Eastern practices is that you learn to check in with your body. Are you slouching? Are you remembering to breathe? Being aware of your tension can help you relax and be present. The physical symptoms of stress can dissipate when you relax, and this greatly contributes to how clear-headed and focused you are when dealing with your work and other people.

How you hold yourself also affects how you are perceived. I remember a graduate school professor I had who I am sure was very knowledgeable, yet all I remember is a man who reminded me of the singer Joe Cocker, a loose array of flailing arms and legs. His awkward discomfort in his own body is what I picked up on, not the information he tried to impart.

When you convey presence, you are perceived as a good listener, and people will share valuable information. In Laurie Nichols's first 90 days in her leadership position, she met with each of her new direct reports. She really wanted to get a feel for their needs and challenges. As an introvert this was demanding for her, but she did it. Later she commented, "Maybe introverts have to work harder because all this total individual one-on-one stuff takes energy. I mean, to invest the time and energy in building those relationships in a way that is comfortable for you, that's more work. It would be easier to not feel like you have to do that, but the real value is by the time you are finished with all that, you've gained a level of trust that maybe the extrovert wouldn't have." Laurie pushed herself, and feels that the payoff was increased trust. As a leader you can't ask for much more.

By increasing your presence, you are also creating a strong web of relationships that allow you to work through others to achieve results. My COO (with the great listening skills) was able to successfully manage a transformational change project that shook up an entire company by building on the trust she had built up. People wanted to work on her team because of the respect she had earned.

Push

What are some of the key payoffs of push? Becoming more visible is one significant benefit of pushing yourself to emerge from the shadows. Groucho Marx said 90 percent of success is just showing up. By pushing yourself to be more engaged, you will achieve more personal power and influence. It can also help your career as you become the person that people think of when they need a specific talent. Salespeople call it being "top of mind." You will become the "go to" person.

Preparation helps you push yourself in new directions. You don't always need a full-blown plan to get results, but some preparation does help. This next example illustrates the old adage, "Opportunity is where luck meets preparation." At a networking event that Martin Schmidler had prepared for, he decided to start a conversation with someone at the cocktail reception. As luck would have it, a person from one of the companies he wanted to learn more about joined the conversation. He had prepared by reading up on the company, and asked the individual to introduce him to the CEO. Martin knew that he was very involved in community service. After the event, Martin followed up with the CEO and easily secured an appointment. He is proud of this result, and knows that without a good push to himself, this payoff would never have occurred.

Several years ago, I interviewed Heather Schulz, a management consultant and co-author with Chip Bell of *Dance Lessons: Six Steps* to *Great Partnerships in Business and Life*,[1] and she illustrated another benefit of push. In finding a mentor, she said that you should seek out the absolutely best person in tha area you want to learn. Heather said that too many of us are reluctant to take the risk of asking. She walked her talk. When Heather was exploring management consulting as a career she decided to contact Tom Peters, who was the guru in that world. Fast-forward to several years later, and Heather was running his company as CEO and president!

Practice

Practice is the one step that addresses *all* the challenges of being an introverted leader: stress, perception gaps, career derailers, and invisibility. Several introverts told me of painful experiences they had as a child because of their lack of social initiative. One was almost left back in first grade because she never spoke and teachers thought she was "slow." Another introvert told me, "If you can survive being a quiet teenager, you can pretty much make it anywhere." Another learned to ask girls out as a way to conquer his fear. Introverts have a history of practicing to adjust to an outgoing society. It is no different when they become adults in the workplace.

Everyone I spoke with discussed the value of practicing. Martin Schmidler combats the perception that he is a slow thinker when asked to respond to a request. Martin says that it is all about how he "frames it up." He wants to be seen as a thoughtful, reflective person rather than a procrastinator or indecisive. He closes the perception gap when he tells people, "These are very good ideas. I need some time to think about them and absorb them and then I will get back to you tomorrow morning or this afternoon." He is very specific about when he will respond, and he follows through on this commitment. He learned through practice to do this.

One of my favorite, colorful, fashion experts is Tim Gunn. He stars in the hit Bravo television show *Project Runway* and is chief creative officer at Liz Claiborne Inc. He encourages designers who compete in a contest each week with a simple coaching statement, "Make it work." That clear statement has the right amount of push and practice philosophy embedded in it. He is saying that you know you can do this, and acknowledging that also takes effort. In an interview, Mr. Gunn discussed the art of small talk[2] He said that when he started teaching at the Parsons New School for Design he was so terrified that he braced his back against the wall in order to stand. He said he got over his fear by becoming a good actor and practicing. He advises his students to do the same. This skill now appears to be effortless for him.

Practicing can take some pretty interesting forms. Paul Otte said that when speaking, "I often wear a nice suit and imagine that this is a suit of armor, or like Ronald Reagan, a Teflon suit where whatever eggs and tomatoes they throw I am invincible. Another coping mechanism, I suppose." Practicing is how habits get formed, and once one skill is under your belt, it's on to more practice in other areas. Learning and growth is a continual process.

As an introverted leader, once you can jump the hurdles outlined in chapters 4–9, you will open up career opportunities, create visibility, and gain a tremendous sense of confidence.

So far in this chapter, we have discussed the numerous personal payoffs of putting the 4 P's in place. There are also other benefits. You are not the only one who stands to win when you adopt the 4 P's. Your organization also reaps the benefits as you share your heart, mind, and potential with others. Let's step back and take a look at what specific wins there are for your organization when you build upon your quiet strength.

Wins for Your Organization

Prepare

Introverted leaders who prepare for dialogues and research their stakeholders' needs build trust and commitment with employees, customers, and managers. By having a game plan for your interactions, you can achieve higher levels of performance, which translates into performance results for your organization.

Several years ago, one of my clients had an associate named Rosanna who attended a number of training programs. I knew that budgets were tight, so I asked her how she had secured approval for so many of these. She explained to me that she had made a business case for each of these programs, laying out detailed outcomes and explaining how investing in these courses would help her to achieve departmental and individual goals. In addition to her careful analysis, part of her preparation included observing the best times to approach her boss. She also offered to share her learning with the staff. Preparation was Rosanna's key to securing results. She continues to be seen as a valuable player, and has been promoted several times in the last few years.

In the earlier example of Martin Schmidler's networking experience, careful preparation and background research on the company and CEO he was targeting, as well as his own push to himself, opened the door to a fruitful interchange and ultimately a new account for his company. Bottom-line results like this occurred from applying the 4 P's.

Presence

Leaders who have presence are able to relate to employees more effectively, and can be more effective in getting the job done. Waldo Waldman, a former fighter pilot and motivational speaker, believes that leaders must "walk the flight line" and get out with their "troops" to learn what is really going on. He asks, "Do you know their issues, gripes, and personal concerns? Do you know what gets in the way of them giving their best? . . . When you know the job details and understand the challenges your wingmen face, you'll be far better prepared to deal with human resource issues such as hiring, firing, and job moves." Waldo believes that you can build relationships at any level of the organization.[3]

Having presence also connects to how well teams work together. Many of today's best corporate leadership development programs emphasize a team approach to getting work done. Jeff Immelt, CEO of GE, described the reason for this evolution into learning to work with others. In an article in *Fortune* magazine,[4] he said, "At the GE I grew up in, most of my training was individually based. That led to problems." He would get back to work after a 3-week program and be able to use only 60 percent of what he'd learned because he needed others—his boss, his IT guy—to help with the rest. Now GE trains teams together to make business decisions.

There is a strong business case for acting with presence. In the book *Love 'Em or Lose 'Em,* authors Bev Kaye and Sharon Jordan Evans emphasize that one of the key reasons people stay in companies is how they are treated by their bosses.[5] Leaders with presence create a climate in which people are appreciated for their contributions. Companies that are populated with managers who have presence attract and retain employees.

Push

Leaders who push themselves to speak up provide value to their organizations. Companies get a return on investment when leaders contribute their ideas and do not remain silent. Jay A. Conger's landmark article for the *Harvard Business Review* called "The Art of Persuasion"[6] focuses on persuasion as learning and negotiating, not convincing or selling. As an introverted leader you can build on your excellent listening and problem solving skills by pushing yourself to engage. Conger studied both team leaders and senior leaders and found that they were able to establish credibility, frame for common ground, provide evidence, and connect emotionally with their audiences. He cites many examples of how the force of persuasion was artfully executed to achieve tangible business results.

I attended a class on storytelling for corporate leaders this past year. The group was primarily technical mid-level leaders who were there to go beyond PowerPoint and put a little spice into their presentations.

This was not a natural skill for most of the participants, and I surmised most to be in the push phase of the 4 P's process. After learning a few techniques on story construction, they were asked to dig deep. Most surprised themselves. Everyone had some kind of impact on the audience when they spoke. We were occasionally moved to tears, often laughed, and certainly empathized with each unique yet universal tale. I heard from several class members after the class who shared positive results back at work, including increased visibility with senior management and positive responses from peers about their improved presentation style. They learned that pushing themselves past their comfort zone allowed people to hear a clear message. When that message is acted upon, the company reaps the benefits.

Practice

Leaders who continue to refine their people skills help their employees gain resilience during inevitable organizational changes. They also garner respect from others when they model ongoing personal and professional development. On a macro level, as more individuals intentionally step out of the prison of ineffective behaviors they have fallen into and develop ways to use the quiet strength of their introversion, organizations draw from the collective talent of their entire organization. This contributes to a stronger bottom line. The subtitle of the *Fortune* magazine issue on leaders summed it up:

> Your competition can copy every advantage you've got—
> except one. That's why the world's best companies are realiz-
> ing that no matter what business they're in, their real business
> is building leaders.[7]

The financial investment in leadership development programs at leading companies is evidence of this strong trend. They have support from senior levels of the organization, and younger employees seek out companies that offer the chance to learn and practice leadership skills. The programs take place in the classroom, online, and through mentoring and job design. We hear terms such as engagement and inspiration. These leadership skills were formerly thought of as soft skills, yet most companies today recognize the critical importance of these competencies.

But what if you are not in one of these prominent Fortune 100 companies that strive to groom leaders? There are many examples I have seen of smaller, less well-funded organizations that provide tremendous mentoring and community service opportunities to their employees. Smaller organizations offer more opportunities to push and practice new people skills. You can push yourself to facilitate a meeting when the CEO is traveling. A customer stops in and the account manager is out? No problem. You can meet with them. Did you just learn some new functionality of the software system? You can offer to do a lunch-and-learn training session for the staff. The organization benefits by having a fluid array of staff who can step into new roles at a moment's notice. Companies increase their bench strength or capable talent through the initiative you take by consciously stepping out and practicing.

There are both personal and organizational payoffs from using the 4 P's Process to enhance your people skills. Now, lets look at the impact of trying too hard to change.

Trying Too Hard to Change

Jungian psychology has a concept called the shadow or dark side. This aspect of ourselves emerges when we are under stress. As you work on stepping out of your introverted self to lead more effectively, it is possible that in your willingness to change you will try too hard. Overusing any of the 4 P's can ricochet and yield negative results. For instance, too much preparation is possible. You may remember being unsure of material for a test you studied for back in school. Didn't you find that the more you studied, the more confusing it became? It is the same with prepping for a meeting, conversation, or networking event. Preparation reaches a point of no return, and you can feel anxious and start to second-guess yourself.

It is also possible to go overboard on presence. As we have said, it is very common for introverted people to act the role of a sociable person. In fact, many actors and comedians are admitted introverts. Johnny Carson, the master of late-night television talk, was inept at socializing and avoided people.[8] Pretending to be a confident star or the hostess of a party can be a way to reframe an anxious situation in your head. By imagining, you act "as if" and behave in a more outgoing manner. Yet, playing a part can also backfire, if you act so that others see you as being too "on." Asking a barrage of questions, making the conversation all about you, or laughing too often or too loudly exhausts you and the people with whom you are trying to connect.

Can you push yourself too hard? I teach 3-day people skills seminars for technically oriented managers. It is a jam-packed 3 days, with lots of skill practice, role plays, and problem solving around people issues. Many of the participants are waking up parts of their brains that are there but not often used. Inevitably, midway through these programs I get the deer-in-headlights expression. I then usually lighten up the discussion, slow down the pace, and switch to content that is more comfortable for them. For instance, they practice active listening by talking about a software problem. Excessively pushing yourself out of your comfort zone can lead to too much emphasis on weak areas. This just makes it harder to learn.

Waldo Waldman, who I mentioned earlier, references his flying days when his squadron used the expression "push it up" to mean to be ready to fly at a moment's notice. He wants people to always be ready for peak performance. I also believe there are times when push it *down* is appropriate. Continuously trying too hard can lead to exhaustion and feelings of self-defeat. You can start to believe that you will never get this "people stuff," and if that happens you are likely to give up.

We have said that practice is the key to success in dealing with an extroverted world. Yet you can also practice so much that you come across as inauthentic to others. I worked at a university where the provost was seen as unapproachable. He rarely came out of his office, and when he did, he spoke only to his inner circle. Each year he hosted a gala holiday party at his home that we were all implicitly required to attend. Each year he would welcome us with a tight smile on his face. The problem was, the smile did not leave his face. Not ever, even when you were talking about something serious. He came across as not being genuine or authentic. My best guess is that no amount of practice at seeming friendly would have helped this provost. He would have been better off practicing less at this holiday party and integrating some other nonverbal components into his repertoire throughout the year. Other suggestions for the smiling provost and others are detailed in chapter 5, Managing and Leading.

James Copeland, CEO of Deloitte Touche Tohmatsu, admitted to being insecure in social settings. He said he just toughed it out and did the best he could. He dealt with his weakness by being active in endeavors such as the United Way, where there was a problem to be solved. Most likely, practice would not change this discomfort so he was wise to focus his efforts on settings where he could shine.[9]

Chapter 11

What's Next? Moving Toward Success

The scene was the CIO retirement party. A simple wine and cheese reception, including a few tributes and a gift presentation, was planned to honor a well-liked man who had given more than 20 years of service. Zach, a junior network administrator, entered the party smiling. He was pleased to have a chance to pay homage to the man who mentored him. Calling people by name, he found his way over to the CIO, met his family, and congratulated him. Zach then moved through the buffet line and around the room, introducing people to each other. He told an amusing anecdote to the group. After an hour at the party, he felt satisfied because he had honored this man he respected, had reconnected with people, and had met some new ones. As he walked out of the party, the division vice president pulled Zach aside. The VP encouraged him to apply for a new position several levels above his current one.

In observing these events, few people would guess that Zach was actually very introverted. Indeed, there was a time not too long before that party that Zach hyperventilated at the thought of attending a business reception. Fortunately, he had applied the 4 P's Process to this situation and came out a winner. What did he do?

Preparation

When he saw the reception on his calendar, Zach prepared for it as he would any work assignment. In addition to his mentor, Zach thought about who would likely be attending and set a goal to talk to five of those people and connect at least three of them with each other.

Presence

Zach was aware of how important his body language and nonverbal cues were in how he was perceived. He took slow, deep breaths, relaxed his shoulders, and put on a genuine smile. As people spoke to him, he looked into their eyes. He moved on politely when there was a break in the conversation.

Push

Zach had a large project deadline looming. He could have easily stayed at his work station and focused on this priority. But he also knew that he had to step out of what was comfortable and familiar. Though the results of socializing might not be as tangible as his deliverables and project milestones, the investment would pay off in rewards such as increased visibility and recognition. In his case, a potential job opportunity arose because he was on the radar screen of the VP who also attended the reception.

Practice

Zach practiced the answers to questions he might be asked at the reception, and wrote down a list of conversation starters he could bring with him. He tried these out on friends and colleagues in other social situations. This made it much easier when the actual event occurred.

Create Your 4 P's Action Plan

So what can you do to create your success story? Setting specific goals for which you are accountable will move your leadership to the next level.

1. Turn to your sticky note on page XXX. You identified some possible improvement areas from the *Introverted Leader Quiz*. Take a moment to write two to three of the areas you identified

for improvement in the first column on the left in the Sample Plan in Figure 18.

2. Turn to the last page of each chapter (chapters 3–9) that addresses your improvement area. In the next column, under Action Item, list two to three specific actions you will take to improve.

3. In the third column, Success Measure, indicate how you will measure completion of the goal.

4. Next, indicate your sources of support. This includes the people in your circle of support.

5. Finally, list the completion date. This gives you a definite target to aim for.

See the sample plan below.

Figure 18. Sample Plan

Improve-ment Area	Action Item	Success Measure	Sources of Support	By When
Managing	Delegate completion of the Alpha report to John.	John will produce a report that is of high quality.	My boss, Rashid My coach, Augusta	I will begin coaching John today and complete the transfer of work by Friday, 5/30.
0.				
1.				
2.				
3.				
4.				
5.				

Next Steps

If you believe it you can achieve it. Writing down your goals cements your declaration. It says, "I am committing to this change." Consider posting your 4 P's Action Plan in a visible place. Create a spreadsheet or a diagram with them.

Visit www.theintrovertedleader.com for many more tools and ideas. Contribute to our blog discussion to share your progress and challenges in moving forward.

I hope you have gained a few new perspectives and practical tools to apply. As you build on your quiet strength and take hold of your leadership role, you will not be required to change your personality. It will mean that you gain confidence and courage as you step out of the shadows. You and many others will be grateful you did.

Notes

Preface

1. Kahlil Gibran, *The Prophet* (Alfred Knopf, 1968), p. 60.

Introduction

1. Del Jones, "Not All Successful CEO's Are Extroverts," *USA Today,* December 8, 2006.

2. A. L. Hammer and C. R. Martin, *Estimated Frequencies of the Types in the United States Population,* 3rd ed. (Training Handout, Center for Applications of Psychological Type, 2003).

3. Jim Collins, *Good to Great* (Collins, 2001), p. 39.

4. Edward Prewitt, "Management Report. Why IT Leaders Fail," *CIO Magazine,* August 1, 2005.

5. Daniel Goleman, *Social Intelligence* (Bantam Dell, 2006), p. 277.

Chapter 1

1. John Gray, Ph.D., *Mars and Venus in the Workplace* (Harper Collins, 2002), p. 83.

2. Thom Hartmann, *Cracking the Code* (Berrett-Koehler, 2007).

3. Jonathon Rauch, "Caring for Your Introvert," *The Atlantic Monthly,* March 2003, http://theatlantic.com/doc/2003003/rauch (accessed March 1, 2008).

4. *The Infinite Mind: Shyness,* December 26, 2001, Lichtenstein Creative Media.

Chapter 2

1. *The Pursuit of Happyness,* directed by Gabriel Muccino, Sony Pictures, 2006.

Chapter 4

1. *Buffet and Gates Go Back to School,* PBS Home Video Net Foundation for Television, 2006.

2. Annette Simmons, *Whoever Tells the Best Story Wins* (AMACOM, 2007), p. 4.

3. Renee Grant Williams, *Voice Power* (AMACOM, 2002), p. 23.

4. Renee Grant Williams, *Voice Power* (AMACOM, 2002), p. 66.

Chapter 5

1. George L. Hanbury, Alka Sapat, and Charles W. Washington, "Know Yourself and Take Charge of Your Own Destiny: The Fit Model of Leadership," *Public Administration Review*, Sept.–Oct. 2004, vol. 64 no. 5.

2. Daniel Goleman, *Social Intelligence* (Bantam Dell, 2006), p. 277.

3. Liz Clamen interviews Warren Buffet, CNBC, December 4, 2006.

4. Stewart Stokes, "Managing the Toughest Transition," *Information Systems Management*, Spring, Part I (2003), p. 8–13.

5. Bill Kahnweiler and Jennifer B. Kahnweiler, *Shaping Your HR Role: Succeeding in Today's Organizations* (Elsevier, 2005).

6. Alan Horowitz, "The Leader Within," *ComputerWorld*, October 2007, p. 1.

7. Markus Buckingham, *The One Thing You Need to Know: about Great Managing, Great Leading, and Sustained Individual Success* (Free Press, 2005).

8. Stewart Stokes, "Managing the Toughest Transition," *Information Systems Management*, Spring, Part I (2003), p. 8–13.

9. Daniel Pink, *A Whole New World: Why Right Brainers Will Rule the Future* (Riverhead Books, 2006), p. 154.

10. Daniel Goleman, *Social Intelligence* (Bantam Dell, 2006), p. 277.

11. Stephen Covey, *The Seven Habits of Highly Effective People* (Free Press, 1990).

12. Nelson Mandela, "His Eight Lessons of Leadership," *Time Magazine*, June 21, 2008.

13. Malcolm Gladwell, *Blink: The Power of Thinking without Thinking* (Little Brown, 2005).

14. Paul Ekman, *Emotions Revealed* (Owl Books, 2003).

Chapter 6

1. Project Management Institute, www.pmi.org.

2. *Curb Your Enthusiasm*, directed by Robert B. Weide, HBO, November 25, 2001.

3. Shannon Kalvar, comment on "Passing as an Extrovert," the Tech Republic Blog, comment posted November 11, 2007.www.blogs. techrepublic.com/project-management (accessed January 2009).

4. N. Gorla and Yan Wah Lam, "Who Should Work with Whom? Building Effective Software Project Teams," *Communications of the ACM*, 2004, vol. 47 no. 6.

5. N. Gorla and Yan Wah Lam, "Who Should Work with Whom? Building Effective Software Project Teams," *Communications of the ACM*, 2004, vol. 47 no. 6.

6. Chester Elton, "The Carrot Principle, Laughing All the Way to the Bank," *Harvard Business Review,* September 2003, p. 137.

7. Harvard Business School Press online, "Reinventing Project Management," http://www.pmi.org/pages/myth_vs_reality.aspx (accessed November 2008)

8. Daniel Pink, *A Whole New Mind: Why Right Brainers Will Rule the Future* (Riverhead Books, 2006).

9. Fabio Sala, "Laughing All the Way to the Bank," *Harvard Business Review,* September 1, 2003.

10. Dave Hemsath and Jeevan Sivasubramaniam, *301 Ways to Have More Fun at Work* (Berrett-Koehler, 2007).

Chapter 7

1. Peter Drucker, *The Practice of Management* (Collins, 1993).

2. *Office Space*, directed by Mike Judge, 20th Century Fox, 1999.

Chapter 8

1. Stanley Hsu, "A Study by Walter Green, Founder of Harrison Conference Services, Inc. and Hofstra University," *The International Tribune*, 1990.

2. Jessica Guynn, "Silicon Valley Meetings Go 'Topless,'" *Los Angeles Times,* March 31, 2008.

3. Roberto Vargas, *Family Activism: Empowering Your Community, Beginning with Family and Friends* (Berrett-Koehler, 2008).

Chapter 9

1. Jay Conger and N Anand, "Capabilities of the Consummate Networker," *Organizational Dynamics* (2007) vol. 36 no. 1.

2. Jane E. Brody, "Cracking the Code to the Memory Vault," *New York Times,* December 4 2007.

3. Anne Baber and Lynne Waymon, *Make Your Contacts* (AMACOM, 2007), p. 87–88.

4. Sam Horn, *Network Naturally*, 2007, CD, www.samhorn.com.

Chapter 10

1. Chip Bell and Heather Schultz, *Dance Lessons: Six Steps to Great Partnerships in Business and Life* (Berrett-Koehler, 1998).

2. Elva Ramirez, "Makes Small Talk," Style Expert Tim Gunn online. WSJ.com. October 25, 2007.

3. Waldo Waldman website, www.wingman.com.

4. George Colvin, "How Top Companies Breed Stars," *Fortune Magazine,* September 20, 2007, http://money.cnn.com/magazine/fortune/fortune_archive/2007/10/01/100351829/ind.ex.htm (accessed February 2008).

5. Beverly Kaye and Sharon Jordan Evans, *Love 'Em or Lose 'Em: Getting Good People to Stay,* 4th ed. (Berrett-Koehler, 2008).

6. Jay Conger, "The Necessary Art of Persuasion," *Harvard Business Review,* May–June 1998, p. 85–95.

7. George Colvin, "How Top Companies Breed Stars," *Fortune Magazine,* September 20, 2007, http://money.cnn.com/magazine/fortune/fortune_archive/2007/10/01/100351829/ind.ex.htm. (accessed February 2008).

8. Mark Rahner, "Johnny Carson: A Former Mrs. Carson Releases the Classic Johnny Carson Show on DVD," http://www.seattletimes.nwsource.com, March 2, 2007.

9. Del Jones, "Not All Successful CEO's Are Extroverts," *USA Today,* December 8, 2006.

Acknowledgments

Books don't get written by themselves. I was a conduit for the stories and wisdom I received from the thousands of introverted leaders I have worked with over the years. Special thanks to those of you whom I interviewed who willingly shared your experience. Though I can't list every one of you here, please know that you made this book come alive.

I am so fortunate to have a tight family circle. Thank you to my husband, best friend, and rock of 35 years, Bill Kahnweiler, who deserves the Nobel prize of author spouses. As I rode the roller coaster of this experience, your love supported me. You sacrificed weekends, cooked me fabulous meals, and were the voice of reason through every impasse.

I would have been incredulous, if someone told me in the years of teenage drama, that my twenty-something daughters, Lindsey and Jessie, would become my close friends and greatest cheerleaders. I have boundless love for you both and draw strength and joy from the contributions you are making in the world.

Many thanks also to my parents, Lucille and Alvin Boretz, who took pride in every large or small accomplishment I have ever had, showed me that work could bring joy and that creativity and discipline are a winning combination. "Now Alvin get to work!" was a mantra I repeated often to myself over the last 2 years. You also taught me that if you ask the right questions, everyone has an interesting story to tell. To my in-laws, Ruth and Louis Kahnweiler, who have treated me as a daughter and who truly serve their community. Thank you also to my level-headed and loyal aunt Arline Garson; my sister, Carrie Boretz; and my sisters-in-law Nancy Randall and Kathy Kahnweiler; and also Adam Goldberg, my future son-in-law.

I am also indebted to my circle of friends and colleagues for the many layers of your support. Deep appreciation goes to Debbie

Sakagawa and her team, Patti Danos, Linda Robinson, Sam Horn, Marilynn Mobley, C.J. Dorgeloh, Marty Mercer, Amy Krupsky, Bobbie Wunsch, Ruth Kleinrock, Jan Weinberg, Barbara Lebow, Angela Ward, Scott Mastley, Tricia Molloy, Jackie Sherman, Laura Raines, Bill Treasurer, John Kador, and the entire BK Author's Cooperative. Thanks also to my wonderful Saturday morning group, Thursday book club, LEXCI group, and NSA-GA.

I feel uniquely blessed to have Berrett-Koehler as my publisher. Thank you especially to Steve Piersanti, president of Berrett-Koehler, for the honor of partnering with you on this book. You were a true champion of the work and your insights on both a professional and personal level were invaluable. I am a better thinker and writer because of you.

Thank you to executive managing editor Jeevan Sivasubramaniam for advocating for a unique book cover, for your accessibility, and most of all for your sense of humor. Thank you also to Jeremy Sullivan, David Marshall, Maria Jesus Aguilo, Catherine Legronne, Kristin Frantz, Dianne Platner, Bonnie Kaufman, Mike Crowley, Katie Sheehan, and all of the other BK staff who played a part in the book's production. You are collaborators in the true sense of the word.

And finally, thank you to all the composers and musicians on my iTunes playlist who helped inspire me. The Allman Brothers, Peter White, Rick Braun, Richard Stoltzman, Emanuel Ax, and Carlos Nakai were a few who helped my inner introvert rise to the occasion and complete this book.

Index

Working with the Author

jenniferkahnweiler

"Jennifer wowed the group. She has the rare combination of delivering 'news you can use' mixed with humor and authenticity. . . . Both introverts and extroverts alike were buzzing about their insights and next steps long after the meeting ended."
—Heather Rocker, former Executive Director, Women in Technology

Jennifer B. Kahnweiler, PhD, CSP, BCC, is an international speaker and executive coach who helps organizations bring out the best in their introverted talent. Programs include engaging keynote speeches, content-rich full-day seminars and shorter webinars, self-directed learning opportunities, and results-driven group and executive coaching.

Keynote Speeches

- *Quiet Influence: How Introverts Make a Difference*
  The key message of this session is that you don't have to act like an extrovert to make a difference. In this interactive presentation, Jennifer draws upon important lessons from highly effective Quiet Influencers. Participants learn how to make the most of six natural strengths to challenge the status quo, provoke new ways of thinking, effect change, and inspire others to move forward. They will understand how they can capitalize on these strengths by using an online instrument that measures their Quiet Influence Quotient (QIQ). Both introverts and extroverts gain awareness and knowledge from this powerful presentation.

- *The Introverted Leader: Building on Your Quiet Strength*

   In this enlightening and highly engaging program, Jennifer draws upon stories and research from her book of the same name to show how introverts can succeed as leaders and work *with*, not *against*, who they are. Participants learn about the characteristics of introverts, the 4 P's success strategies of introverted leaders, and why our organizations can't afford to miss out on the invaluable contributions of their quieter employees.

In-House Seminars

Jennifer's highly rated workshops take a deep dive into work challenges by applying key tools and principles of introverted leadership and influence. Full-day seminars are The Introverted Leader and Quiet Influence, both of which include content from her popular keynote speeches, self-assessments, workbooks, case studies, and role-plays. She also works with organizations to custom design programs using modules that include Networking, Coaching, Focused Conversations, and Thoughtful Use of Social Media.

Webinars

An expert in the use of distant learning technologies, Jennifer offers webinars that range between one and two hours in length. Webinars are an efficient way of delivering program content in a short period of time while reducing travel costs. Both keynotes and seminar topics can be adapted to this format.

Self-Directed Learning Opportunities

- *Books*

   Print books or digital editions of *Quiet Influence: The Introvert's Guide to Making a Difference* and *The Introverted Leader:*

Building on Your Quiet Strength can be included with all keynote, seminar, and self-directed learning programs at a significantly reduced cost.

• *Learning Bursts*

The Introverted Leader program is available through a unique and innovative learning method called the Learning Burst. Through a partnership with consultant and author Dave Basarab, this process gives participants an opportunity to learn without having to disrupt their daily workflow. A Learning Burst is a combination of a ten-minute audiocast and a workbook of supporting material. The workbook contains easily digestible summaries, quizzes, and exercises to apply and cement the learning points. Audio segments are in MP3 format. For more information, visit our website at www.jenniferkahnweiler.com.

• *PDUs2Go*

We also partner with PDUs2Go and provide several Introverted Leader courses that help project managers meet their Project Management Institute continuing education requirements. Visit www.pdus2go.com to learn more.

Coaching

• *Group Coaching*

Introverted (and extroverted) participants gain great value by discussing provocative questions after seminars and keynotes. Jennifer provides a series of small, extended postsession coaching groups via phone or Skype to give participants an opportunity to engage in focused conversations and problem solving. They share successes, present challenges, receive peer feedback and clear direction in the safe environment she creates. Group coaching also helps the keynote or seminar's messages "stick" in a lasting and meaningful way.

- *Executive Coaching*

  Jennifer B. Kahnweiler, PhD, is a Board Certified Coach with more than twenty-five years of experience providing one-on-one coaching to professionals around the world. She specializes in bringing out the strengths of introverted professionals who want to develop their leadership and influencing skills. Clients appreciate her "velvet hammer" approach, which includes equal doses of support and challenge.

Contact Information

To learn more, visit www.jenniferkahnweiler.com or send an email to info@jenniferkahnweiler.com. Become part of her Quiet Influence community by following her on Twitter (JennKahnweiler), connecting with her on Linked In (Jennifer Kahnweiler), and liking her on Facebook (*Quiet Influence* and *The Introverted Leader* pages).

About the Author

Jennifer Kahnweiler, PhD, is an author, speaker, and executive coach who has been hailed as a "champion for introverts." Her bestselling book *The Introverted Leader: Building on Your Quiet Strength* achieved widespread appeal and has been translated into six languages including Chinese and Spanish.

Her thirty-five-year journey to become an expert on introverts included jobs as an elementary school counselor, university administrator, federal government program director, and career coach. She also deepened her knowledge of and appreciation for introverts through her work as a learning and development professional inside leading organizations such as GE, AT&T, NASA, Turner Broadcasting, and the CDC. Jennifer became committed to championing quieter people, first by helping organizations recognize and value them, and second, by helping introverted individuals step confidently into leadership and influencing roles.

Through keynote speeches and seminars on the topic that include her characteristic humor, poignant stories, and practical tools, she transfers the lessons introverts teach us. Jennifer has also written articles about introverts in the workplace for *Forbes*, *Bloomberg Businessweek*, and the *Wall Street Journal* and has been quoted on the subject in more than fifty international news media outlets, including the *New York Times* and *Time* magazine's January 2012 cover story on introverts.

Jennifer received her doctorate in counseling and organizational development at Florida State University and her earlier degrees in sociology and counseling at Washington University in St. Louis. She is a recipient of the 2012 Certified Speaking Professional (CSP) award, the National Speakers Association's highest earned designation. She has also served on the board of the Berrett-Koehler Author's Co-op and is on the board of the National Speakers Association of Georgia, where she heads up the community service program.

Truth be told, though, the greatest inspiration for her work with introverts has been her forty-year marriage to her husband, Bill. It has been said that couples start to resemble each other after a period of time. Over these four decades, Jennifer has indeed embraced some of Bill's introverted tendencies and developed her own quiet strengths.

She is the grateful mother of children Jessie, Lindsey, and Adam. Though she is happy to call Atlanta, Georgia, home, her native New York will always be "the city." She adores yoga (except the hot kind), can turn shopping into an art form, and appreciates any chance to escape to an amazing Korean spa off of I-85. Her most surprising lifetime about-face involves feline friends. She wrote in her high school yearbook that she "hated" cats. And today? She savors quiet time with Fred, the Kahnweiler cat (even though he likes Bill better).

Also by Jennifer Kahnweiler

Quiet Influence
The Introvert's Guide to Making a Difference

Introverts may feel powerless in a world where extroverts seem to rule, but there's more than one way to have some sway. Jennifer Kahnweiler proves introverts can be highly effective influencers when, instead of trying to act like extroverts, they use their natural strengths. Kahnweiler identifies six unique strengths introverts have and includes a Quiet Influence Quotient quiz to measure how well you're using these six strengths now. Then, through questions, tools, exercises, and real-world examples, she helps you increase your mastery of these strengths.

"This extraordinary book shows that you don't have to raise your volume to have a voice."

—Susan Cain, author of *Quiet: The Power of Introverts in a World That Can't Stop Talking*

Paperback, 192 pages, ISBN 978-1-60994-562-6
PDF ebook, ISBN 978-1-60994-563-3

BK Berrett–Koehler Publishers, Inc.
San Francisco, *www.bkconnection.com*   **800.929.2929**

Berrett–Koehler
Publishers

Berrett–Koehler
Publishers

A community dedicated to creating
a world that works for all

Visit Our Website: www.bkconnection.com

Read book excerpts, see author videos and Internet movies, read
our authors' blogs, join discussion groups, download book apps, find
out about the BK Affiliate Network, browse subject-area libraries of
books, get special discounts, and more!

Subscribe to Our Free E-Newsletter, the *BK Communiqué*

Be the first to hear about new publications, special discount offers,
exclusive articles, news about bestsellers, and more! Get on the list
for our free e-newsletter by going to **www.bkconnection.com**.

Get Quantity Discounts

Berrett-Koehler books are available at quantity discounts for orders
of ten or more copies. Please call us toll-free at (800) 929-2929 or
email us at bkp.orders@aidcvt.com.

Join the BK Community

BKcommunity.com is a virtual meeting place where people from
around the world can engage with kindred spirits to create a world
that works for all. BKcommunity.com members may create their own
profiles, blog, start and participate in forums and discussion groups,
post photos and videos, answer surveys, announce and register for
upcoming events, and chat with others online in real time. Please join
the conversation!

Certified

Corporation
bcorporation.net

The Foolish Turtle

ISBN 0-7696-4040-0

50395

EAN

School Specialty
Children's Publishing

Library of Congress-in-Publication Data is on file with the publisher.

Send all inquires to:
8720 Orion Place
Columbus, OH 43240-2111

ISBN 0-7696-4040-0

1 2 3 4 5 6 7 8 9 10 EVN 10 09 08 07 06 05 04

The Foolish Turtle

By Anna Wilson

Illustrated by Mike Gordon

GINGHAM DOG
PRESS

Columbus, Ohio

"I wish I could fly,"
said Terry.
Polly laughed.

5

"Why are you laughing?" asked Terry.
"I want to fly.
I think I can do it."

6

7

Polly laughed and laughed.
"You are a turtle," she said.
"Turtles cannot fly."

19

"I will teach myself to fly," said Terry.
"You will see."

Terry found his friend, Dora.
She could fly.
"I want to fly.
Will you help me?" he asked her.

Dora laughed and
laughed.
"You are a turtle,"
she said.
"Turtles cannot fly."

"But I think I can do it," said Terry.
"Okay," said Dora. "I will help you.
Hold this twig and you will fly."

"How will I fly?" asked Terry.
"You hold one end of the twig," she said.

"I will hold the other.
Together, we will fly."

Dora grabbed the twig.
Terry grabbed the twig.

Dora flew into the air.
Terry flew into the air.

Polly laughed and laughed.
"Look at Terry," she said.
"He looks silly in the air."

Terry was angry.

He let go of the twig.

"I do not look silly!" he yelled.

"I am flying!"

27

Terry began to fall.
He fell down
through the air.

Splash!

29

Terry fell into the pond.

"You sure look silly now!" said Polly.

"Maybe," said Terry, "but at least I was
able to fly!"

Words I Know

fly   look

found   said

help   want

hold   will

Think About It!

1. What did Terry want to teach himself?
2. Why did Terry's friends laugh at him?
3. How did Dora help Terry to fly?
4. Why did Terry fall into the pond?
5. Terry learned an important lesson at the end of the story. What do you think Terry learned?

The Story and You

1. How do you think Terry felt when his friends laughed at him?
2. How do you feel when people laugh at you?
3. Have you ever wanted to do something that other people thought was impossible?